CW00548037

PRESENTED TO

_____

PRESENTED BY

_____

DATE

_____

OCCASION

PRESENTED TO

PRESENTED BY

DATE

OCCASION

IN THE
WORDS OF JESUS

New Living
Translation.

SECOND EDITION

Visit Tyndale online at www.tyndale.com.

TYNDALE and Tyndale's quill logo are registered trademarks of
Tyndale House Publishers, Inc.

In the Words of Jesus

Copyright © 2015 Tyndale House Publishers, Inc. All rights
reserved.

Previously published in 1997 as *Living Words of Jesus* by Tyndale
House Publishers under ISBN 978-0-8423-3249-1.

Packaging textile pattern copyright © touring/iStockphoto. All
rights reserved.

Designed by Mark Anthony Lane II

Scriptures compiled by Mark Norton

Scripture quotations are taken from the *Holy Bible*, New Living
Translation, copyright © 1996, 2004, 2007, 2013 by Tyndale
House Foundation. Used by permission of Tyndale House
Publishers, Inc., Carol Stream, Illinois 60188. All rights reserved.

Notes and Bible Helps copyright © 1988, 1989, 1990, 1991,
1993, 1996, 2004, 2005 by Tyndale House Publishers, Inc. New
Testament Notes and Bible Helps copyright © 1986 owned by
assignment by Tyndale House Publishers, Inc. All rights reserved.

ISBN 978-1-4964-0253-0

Printed in China

21   20   19   18   17   16   15
7   6   5   4   3   2   1

CONTENTS

Love

Forgiveness

Prayer

The Kingdom of God

Other Teachings of Jesus

Warnings of Jesus

Other Illustrations Jesus Used

TO THE READER

WHO IS JESUS? Over the centuries He's been called everything from a wise teacher to a heretic to the Savior of the world.

In this book, we have assembled the words of Jesus primarily from the four books of the Bible that tell the story of His life: the Gospels of Matthew, Mark, Luke, and John. Organized by topic, this book allows you to investigate what Jesus said about Himself and other topics. Short notes after each verse explain the culture, history, and background behind the saying.

Each verse in this book is written in the New Living Translation. Based on the most recent scholarship and theory in translation, the New Living Translation is easy to read and understand while accurately communicating the meaning of the original text.

We hope that Jesus Christ's words will speak to your heart and you will continue your study of His life and work.

ONE SOLITARY LIFE

HE WAS BORN in an obscure village, the child of
a peasant woman. He grew up in another village.
He worked in a carpenter shop until He was
thirty and then for three years was an itinerant
preacher. He never wrote a book. He never held
an office. He never owned a home. He never
traveled two hundred miles from the place where
He was born. He never did one of the things
that usually accompany greatness. He had no
credentials but Himself.

Although He walked the land over, curing
the sick, giving sight to the blind, healing the
lame, and raising people from the dead, the top
established religious leaders turned against Him.
His friends ran away. He was turned over to
enemies. He went through the mockery of a trial.
He was spat upon, flogged, and ridiculed. He
was nailed to a cross between two thieves. While
He was dying, the executioners gambled for the
only piece of property He had on earth, and that
was His robe. When He was dead, He was laid in
a borrowed grave through the pity of a friend.

Nineteen wide centuries have come and
gone, and today He is the central figure

of the human race and the Leader of the column of progress.

All the armies that ever marched, and all the navies that were ever built, and all the parliaments that ever sat, and all the kings that ever reigned, put together, have not affected the life of man upon this earth as has that One Solitary Life.

—*Source Unknown*

THE PERSON
OF JESUS

The Identity of Jesus

"I am the bread of life. Whoever comes to me will never be hungry again. Whoever believes in me will never be thirsty. But you haven't believed in me even though you have seen me. However, those the Father has given me will come to me, and I will never reject them. For I have come down from heaven to do the will of God who sent me, not to do my own will. And this is the will of God, that I should not lose even one of all those he has given me, but that I should raise them up at the last day. For it is my Father's will that all who see his Son and believe in him should have eternal life. I will raise them up at the last day."

JOHN 6:35-40

REFLECTION

Jesus did not work independently of God the Father, but in union with Him. This should give us even more assurance of being welcomed into God's presence and being protected by Him. Jesus' purpose was to do the will of God, not to satisfy Jesus' human desires. When we follow Jesus, we should have the same purpose.

"I am the light of the world. If you follow me, you won't have to walk in darkness, because you will have the light that leads to life."

JOHN 8:12

REFLECTION

Jesus was speaking in the treasury—the part of the Temple where the offerings were put and where candles burned to symbolize the pillar of fire that led the people of Israel through the wilderness. In this context, Jesus called Himself the Light of the World. The pillar of fire represented God's presence, protection, and guidance. Likewise, Jesus brings God's presence, protection, and guidance. Is He the Light of *your* world?

"I have come as a light to shine in this dark world, so that all who put their trust in me will no longer remain in the dark."

JOHN 12:46

REFLECTION

As a soldier follows his captain, so we should follow Christ, our Commander. As a slave follows his master, so we should follow Christ, our Lord. As we follow the advice of a trusted counselor, so we should follow Jesus' commands to us in Scripture. As we follow the laws of our nation, so we should follow the laws of the Kingdom of Heaven.

"I tell you the truth, I am the gate for the sheep. All who came before me were thieves and robbers. But the true sheep did not listen to them. Yes, I am the gate. Those who come in through me will be saved. They will come and go freely and will find good pastures."

JOHN 10:7-9

REFLECTION

In the sheepfold, the shepherd functioned as a gate, letting the sheep in and protecting them. Jesus is the gate to God's salvation for us. He offers access to safety and security. Christ is our protector. Some people resent that Jesus is the gate, the only way of access to God. But Jesus is God's Son—why should we seek any other way or want to customize a different approach to God?

"I am the good shepherd. The good shepherd sacrifices his life for the sheep. A hired hand will run when he sees a wolf coming. He will abandon the sheep because they don't belong to him and he isn't their shepherd. And so the wolf attacks them and scatters the flock. The hired hand runs away because he's working only for the money and doesn't really care about the sheep.

"I am the good shepherd; I know my own sheep, and they know me, just as my Father knows me and I know the Father. So I sacrifice my life for the sheep."

JOHN 10:11-15

REFLECTION

A hired hand tends the sheep for money, while the shepherd does it out of love. The shepherd owns the sheep and is committed to them. Jesus is not merely doing a job; He is committed to love us and has laid down His life for us. False teachers and false prophets do not have this commitment.

"I am the resurrection and the life. Anyone who believes in me will live, even after dying. Everyone who lives in me and believes in me will never ever die. Do you believe this, Martha?"

JOHN 11:25-26

REFLECTION

Jesus has power over life and death as well as power to forgive sins. This is because He is the Creator of life. He who *is* life can surely restore life. Whoever believes in Christ has a spiritual life that death cannot conquer or diminish in any way. When we realize His power and how wonderful His offer to us really is, how can we not commit our lives to Him?

"I am the way, the truth, and the life. No one can come to the Father except through me. If you had really known me, you would know who my Father is. From now on, you do know him and have seen him!"

JOHN 14:6-7

REFLECTION

Jesus says He is the *only* way to God the Father. Some people may argue that this way is too narrow. In reality, it is wide enough for the whole world, if the world chooses to accept it. Instead of worrying about how limited it sounds to have only one way, we should be saying, "Thank You, God, for providing a sure way to get to You!"

"If you trust me, you are trusting not only me, but also God who sent me. For when you see me, you are seeing the one who sent me."

JOHN 12:44-45

REFLECTION

We often wonder what God is like. How can we know the Creator when He doesn't make Himself visible? Jesus said plainly that those who see Him see God, because He *is* God. If you want to know what God is like, study the person and words of Jesus Christ.

"I am the true grapevine, and my Father is the gardener. He cuts off every branch of mine that doesn't produce fruit, and he prunes the branches that do bear fruit so they will produce even more. You have already been pruned and purified by the message I have given you. Remain in me, and I will remain in you. For a branch cannot produce fruit if it is severed from the vine, and you cannot be fruitful unless you remain in me.

"Yes, I am the vine; you are the branches. Those who remain in me, and I in them, will produce much fruit. For apart from me you can do nothing."

JOHN 15:1-5

REFLECTION

Christ is the vine, and God is the Gardener who cares for the branches to make them fruit-ful. The branches are all those who claim to be followers of Christ. The fruitful branches are true believers who by their living union with Christ produce much fruit. But those who don't bear fruit—those who turn back from following Christ after making a superficial commitment—will be separated from the vine. Unfruitful followers are as good as dead and will be cut off and tossed aside.

"Do you believe in the Son of Man? . . . You have seen him, . . . and he is speaking to you!"

JOHN 9:35-37

REFLECTION

The "Son of Man" is Jesus Himself. This title occurs many times in the New Testament in reference to Jesus as the Messiah.

"My Kingdom is not an earthly kingdom. If it were, my followers would fight to keep me from being handed over to the Jewish leaders. But my Kingdom is not of this world."

JOHN 18:36

REFLECTION

In this verse, Jesus is responding to Pilate. Pilate asked Jesus a straightforward question, and Jesus answered clearly. There seems to have been no question in Pilate's mind that Jesus spoke the truth and was innocent of any crime. It also seems apparent that, while recognizing the truth, Pilate chose to reject it. It is a tragedy when we fail to recognize the truth. It is a greater tragedy when we recognize the truth but fail to heed it.

Jesus and the Father

"I tell you the truth, the Son can
do nothing by himself. He does
only what he sees the Father doing.
Whatever the Father does, the Son
also does. For the Father loves the
Son and shows him everything he is
doing. In fact, the Father will show
him how to do even greater works
than healing this man. Then you
will truly be astonished. For just as
the Father gives life to those he raises
from the dead, so the Son gives life
to anyone he wants."

JOHN 5:19-21

REFLECTION
Because of His unity with God, Jesus lived as God wanted Him to live. Because of our identification with Jesus, we must honor Him and live as He wants us to live. The question "What would Jesus do?" may help us make the right choices.

"Since you don't know who I am, you don't know who my Father is. If you knew me, you would also know my Father."

JOHN 8:19

REFLECTION
Jesus and the Father are one.

"The Father and I are one."

JOHN 10:30

REFLECTION

This is the clearest statement of Jesus' divinity He ever made. Jesus and His Father are not the same person, but they are one in essence and nature. Thus, Jesus is not merely a good teacher— He is God. His claim to be God was unmistakable. The religious leaders wanted to kill Him because their laws said that anyone claiming to be God should die. Nothing could persuade them that Jesus' claim was true.

"I tell you the truth, anyone who welcomes my messenger is welcoming me, and anyone who welcomes me is welcoming the Father who sent me."

JOHN 13:20

REFLECTION

When people welcome our proclamations of the Good News, they are also welcoming Jesus Christ and, through Him, the Father.

"Have I been with you all this time, Philip, and yet you still don't know who I am? Anyone who has seen me has seen the Father! So why are you asking me to show him to you? Don't you believe that I am in the Father and the Father is in me? The words I speak are not my own, but my Father who lives in me does his work through me. Just believe that I am in the Father and the Father is in me. Or at least believe because of the work you have seen me do."

JOHN 14:9-11

REFLECTION

Jesus is the visible, tangible image of the invisible God. He is the complete revelation of what God is like. Jesus explained to Philip, who wanted to see the Father, that to know Jesus is to know God. The search for God, for truth and reality, ends in Christ.

The Authority of Jesus

"Is it easier to say 'Your sins are forgiven,' or 'Stand up and walk'? So I will prove to you that the Son of Man has the authority on earth to forgive sins." Then Jesus turned to the paralyzed man and said, "Stand up, pick up your mat, and go home!"

MATTHEW 9:5-6

REFLECTION

It's easy to tell someone his sins are forgiven; it's a lot more difficult to reverse a case of paralysis! Jesus backed up His words by healing the man's legs. Jesus' action showed that His words were true: He had the power to forgive as well as to heal. Talk is cheap, but our words lack meaning if our actions do not back them up. We can say we love God or others, but if we are not taking practical steps to demonstrate that love, our words are empty and meaningless.

"Haven't you read in the law of Moses that the priests on duty in the Temple may work on the Sabbath? . . . For the Son of Man is Lord, even over the Sabbath!"

MATTHEW 12:5, 8

REFLECTION

When Jesus said He was Lord of the Sabbath, He claimed to be greater than the law and above the law. To the Pharisees, this was heresy. They did not realize that Jesus, the divine Son of God, had created the Sabbath. The Creator is always greater than His creation; thus, Jesus had the authority to overrule their traditions and regulations.

"Don't you realize that I could ask my Father for thousands of angels to protect us, and he would send them instantly? But if I did, how would the Scriptures be fulfilled that describe what must happen now?"

MATTHEW 26:53-54

REFLECTION

Jesus said this in response to Peter, who had cut off the servant's ear in Gethsemane. Peter was trying to prevent what he saw as *defeat*. He didn't realize that Jesus had to die in order to gain *victory*. But Jesus demonstrated perfect commitment to His Father's will. His Kingdom would not be advanced with swords but with faith and obedience.

"I can do nothing on my own. I judge as God tells me. Therefore, my judgment is just, because I carry out the will of the one who sent me, not my own will.

"If I were to testify on my own behalf, my testimony would not be valid. But someone else is also testifying about me, and I assure you that everything he says about me is true. In fact, you sent investigators to listen to John the Baptist, and his testimony about me was true. Of course, I have no need of human witnesses, but I say these things so you might be saved. John was like a burning and shining lamp, and you were excited for a while about his message. But I have a greater witness than John—my teachings and my miracles. The Father gave me these works to accomplish, and they prove that he sent me. And the Father who sent me has testified about me himself. You have never heard his voice or seen him face to face, and you do not have his message in your hearts, because you do not believe me—the one he sent to you."

JOHN 5:30-38

REFLECTION
Jesus claimed to be equal with God, to give eternal life, to be the source of life, and to judge sin.

These statements make it clear that Jesus was claiming to be divine—an almost unbelievable claim, but one that was supported by another witness, John the Baptist.

The Mission of Jesus

"Healthy people don't need a doctor—sick people do. . . . Now go and learn the meaning of this Scripture: 'I want you to show mercy, not offer sacrifices.' For I have come to call not those who think they are righteous, but those who know they are sinners."

MATTHEW 9:12-13

REFLECTION

Those who are sure that they are good enough can't be saved, because the first step in following Jesus is acknowledging our need

and admitting that we don't have
all the answers.

"The Spirit of the LORD is upon
    me,
  for he has anointed me to bring
    Good News to the poor.
He has sent me to proclaim that
    captives will be released,
  that the blind will see,
that the oppressed will be set free,
  and that the time of the LORD's
    favor has come. . . .

"The Scripture you've just heard has
been fulfilled this very day!"
LUKE 4:18-21

REFLECTION

Jesus was quoting from Isaiah
61:1-2. Isaiah pictures the deliver-
ance of Israel from exile in
Babylon as a Year of Jubilee when

all debts are canceled, all slaves are freed, and all property is returned to original owners. But the release from Babylonian exile had not brought the expected fulfillment; they were still a conquered and oppressed people. So Isaiah must have been referring to a future messianic age. Jesus boldly announced, "The Scripture you've just heard has been fulfilled this very day!" Jesus was proclaiming Himself as the one who would bring this Good News to pass, but He would do so in a way that the people were not yet able to grasp.

"I have come to set the world on fire, and I wish it were already burning! I have a terrible baptism of suffering ahead of me, and I am under a heavy burden until it is accomplished. Do

you think I have come to bring peace to the earth? No, I have come to divide people against each other! From now on families will be split apart, three in favor of me, and two against—or two in favor and three against.

'Father will be divided against son
   and son against father;
mother against daughter
   and daughter against mother;
and mother-in-law against
      daughter-in-law
   and daughter-in-law against
      mother-in-law.'"

LUKE 12:49-53

REFLECTION

In these strange and unsettling words, Jesus revealed that His coming often results in conflict. Because He demands a response, families may be split apart when some choose to follow Him and others refuse to do so. Jesus allows no middle ground. He demands loyalty and commitment, sometimes to the point of severing other relationships. Are you willing to risk your family's disapproval in order to follow the Lord?

"My nourishment comes from doing the will of God, who sent me, and from finishing his work."
JOHN 4:34

REFLECTION

The "nourishment" about which Jesus was speaking was His spiritual nourishment. It includes more than Bible study, prayer, and attending church. Spiritual nourishment also comes from doing God's will and helping to bring His work of salvation to completion. We are nourished not only by what we take in, but also by what we give out for God.

"My soul is deeply troubled. Should I pray, 'Father, save me from this hour'? But this is the very reason I came! Father, bring glory to your name."

JOHN 12:27-28

REFLECTION

Jesus knew His crucifixion lay ahead, and because He was human, He dreaded it. He knew He would have to take the sins of the world on Himself, and He knew this would separate Him from His Father. He wanted to be delivered from this horrible death, but He knew that God sent Him into the world to die for our sins, in our place. Jesus said no to His human desires in order to obey His Father and glorify Him. Although we will never have to face such a difficult and awesome task, we are still called to obedience. Whatever the Father asks, we should do His will and bring glory to His name.

Jesus and the Children

"Whoever wants to be first must take last place and be the servant of everyone else. . . . Anyone who welcomes a little child like this on my behalf welcomes me, and anyone who welcomes me welcomes not only me but also my Father who sent me."

MARK 9:35-37

REFLECTION

Jesus taught the disciples to welcome children. This was a new approach in a society where children were usually treated as second-class citizens. It is important not only to treat children well but also to teach them about Jesus. Children's ministries should never be regarded as less important than those for adults.

"O Father, Lord of heaven and earth, thank you for hiding these things from those who think themselves wise and clever, and for revealing them to the childlike. Yes, Father, it pleased you to do it this way!"

MATTHEW 11:25-26

REFLECTION

Jesus mentioned two kinds of people in His prayer: the "wise and clever"—arrogant in their own knowledge—and the "childlike"—humbly open to receive the truth of God's Word. Are you wise in your own eyes, or do you seek the truth in childlike faith, realizing that only God holds all the answers?

"I tell you the truth, unless you turn from your sins and become like little children, you will never get into the Kingdom of Heaven. So anyone who becomes as humble as this little child is the greatest in the Kingdom of Heaven."

MATTHEW 18:3-4

REFLECTION

The disciples had become so pre-occupied with the organization of Jesus' earthly Kingdom that they had lost sight of its divine purpose. Instead of seeking a place of service, they sought positions of advantage. It is easy to lose our eternal perspective and compete

for promotions or status in the
church. It is difficult, but healthy,
to identify with "children"—
weak and dependent people with
no status or influence.

"Anyone who welcomes a little child
like this on my behalf is welcoming
me. But if you cause one of these
little ones who trusts in me to fall
into sin, it would be better for you
to have a large millstone tied around
your neck and be drowned in the
depths of the sea."

MATTHEW 18:5-6

REFLECTION

Children are trusting by nature.
Because they trust adults, they
are easily led to faith in Christ.
God holds parents and other
adults accountable for how
they influence these little ones.

Jesus warned that anyone who turns little children away from faith in Him will receive severe punishment.

"Let the children come to me. Don't stop them! For the Kingdom of Heaven belongs to those who are like these children."

MATTHEW 19:14

REFLECTION

Jesus wanted little children to come to Him because He loves them and because they have a guileless trust in God. All people need childlike faith in God. The receptiveness of little children was a great contrast to the stubbornness of the religious leaders, who let their education and sophistication stand in the way of the simple faith needed to believe in Jesus.

The Body and Blood of Jesus

As they were eating, Jesus took some bread and blessed it. Then he broke it in pieces and gave it to the disciples, saying, "Take this and eat it, for this is my body."

And he took a cup of wine and gave thanks to God for it. He gave it to them and said, "Each of you drink from it, for this is my blood, which confirms the covenant between God and his people. It is poured out as a sacrifice to forgive the sins of many. Mark my words—I will not drink wine again until the day I drink it new with you in my Father's Kingdom."

MATTHEW 26:26-29

REFLECTION

Each name we use for this sacrament brings out a different dimension of it. It is the *Lord's Supper* because it commemorates the Passover meal Jesus ate with His disciples; it is the *Eucharist* (thanksgiving) because in it we thank God for Christ's work for us; it is *Communion* because through it we commune with God and with other believers. As we eat the bread and drink the wine, we should be quietly reflective as we recall Jesus' death and His promise to come again, grateful for God's wonderful gift to us, and joyful as we meet with Christ and the body of believers.

"I tell you the truth, Moses didn't give you bread from heaven. My Father did. And now he offers you the true bread from heaven."

JOHN 6:32

REFLECTION

People eat bread to satisfy physical hunger and to sustain physical life. We can satisfy spiritual hunger and sustain spiritual life only by a right relationship with Jesus Christ. No wonder He called Himself the Bread of Life. But bread must be eaten to sustain life, and Christ must be invited into our daily walk to sustain spiritual life.

"I tell you the truth, unless you eat the flesh of the Son of Man and drink his blood, you cannot have eternal life within you. But anyone who eats my flesh and drinks my blood has eternal life, and I will raise that person at the last day. For my flesh is true food, and my blood is true drink. Anyone who eats my flesh and drinks my blood remains in me, and I in him. I live because of the living Father who sent me; in the same way, anyone who feeds on me will live because of me. I am the true bread that came down from heaven. Anyone who eats this bread will not die as your ancestors did (even though they ate the manna) but will live forever."

JOHN 6:53-58

REFLECTION

This was a shocking message— to eat flesh and drink blood sounded cannibalistic. The idea of drinking any blood, let alone human blood, was repugnant to the religious leaders because the law forbade it. Jesus was not talking about literal blood, of course. He was saying that His life had to become their own, but they could not accept this concept. The Gospel writers as well as the apostle Paul used the body and blood imagery in talking about Communion.

FOLLOWING JESUS

FOLLOWING
JESUS

The Call to Follow Jesus

"Come, follow me, and I will show you how to fish for people!"

MARK 1:17

REFLECTION

We often assume that Jesus' disciples were men of great faith from the first time they met Jesus. But they had to grow in their faith just as all believers do. Although it took time for Jesus' call and His message to get through, the disciples *followed*. In the same way, we may question and falter, but we must never stop following Jesus.

"My light will shine for you just a little longer. Walk in the light while you can, so the darkness will not overtake you. Those who walk in the darkness cannot see where they are going. Put your trust in the light while there is still time; then you will become children of the light."

JOHN 12:35-36

REFLECTION

Jesus said He would be with His disciples in person for only a short time, and they should benefit from being in His presence while they had it. Like a light shining in a dark place, He would point out the way they should walk. If they walked in His light, they would become "children of the light," revealing the truth and pointing people to God. As Christians, we are to be Christ's light bearers, letting His light shine through us. How brightly is your light shining? Can others see Christ in your actions?

"You are truly my disciples if you remain faithful to my teachings. And you will know the truth, and the truth will set you free."
JOHN 8:31-32

REFLECTION

Jesus Himself is the truth that sets us free. He is the source of truth, the perfect standard of what is right. He frees us from continued slavery to sin, from self-deception, and from deception by Satan. He shows us clearly the way to eternal life with God. Thus, Jesus does not give us freedom to do what we

want, but freedom to follow
God. As we seek to serve God,
Jesus' perfect truth frees us to
be all that God meant us to be.

The Cost of Following Jesus

"Foxes have dens to live in, and birds have nests, but the Son of Man has no place even to lay his head."

MATTHEW 8:20

REFLECTION

Following Jesus is not always easy or comfortable. Often it means great cost and sacrifice, with no earthly rewards or security. Jesus didn't have a place to call home. You may find that following Christ costs you popularity, friendships, leisure time, or treasured habits. But while the cost of following Christ is high, the value

IN THE WORDS OF JESUS

of being Christ's disciple is even
higher. Discipleship is an investment that lasts for eternity and
yields incredible rewards.

**"Follow me now. Let the spiritually
dead bury their own dead."**
MATTHEW 8:22

REFLECTION

Jesus was always direct with those
who wanted to follow Him. He
made sure they counted the cost
and set aside any conditions they
might have for following Him. As
God's Son, Jesus did not hesitate
to demand complete loyalty. Even
family loyalty was not to take priority over the demands of obedience. His direct challenge forces
us to ask ourselves about our own
priorities in following Him. The
decision to follow Jesus should

not be put off, even though other loyalties compete for our attention. Nothing should be placed above a total commitment to living for Him.

"If you refuse to take up your cross and follow me, you are not worthy of being mine."

MATTHEW 10:38

REFLECTION

To take up our cross and follow Jesus means to be willing to publicly identify with Him, to experience certain opposition, and to be willing to face even suffering and death for His sake.

"If you cling to your life, you will lose it; but if you give up your life for me, you will find it."

MATTHEW 10:39

REFLECTION

This verse is a positive and negative statement of the same truth: clinging to this life may cause us to forfeit the best from Christ in this world *and* in the next. The more we love this life's rewards (leisure, power, popularity, financial security), the more we will discover how empty they really are. The best way to enjoy life, therefore, is to loosen our greedy grasp on earthly rewards so that we can be free to follow Christ. In doing so, we will inherit eternal life and begin at once to experience the benefits of following Christ.

"If any of you wants to be my follower, you must turn from your selfish ways, take up your cross daily, and follow me. If you try to hang on

to your life, you will lose it. But if
you give up your life for my sake, you
will save it. And what do you benefit
if you gain the whole world but are
yourself lost or destroyed?"

LUKE 9:23-25

REFLECTION

To take up the cross meant to
carry one's own cross to the place
of crucifixion. Many Galileans
had been killed that way by the
Romans—and Jesus would face
it as well. With this word picture,
Christ presented a clear and
challenging description of the
Christian life. Being His disciple
means putting aside selfish desires,
shouldering one's cross every day,
and following Him. It is simple
and yet so demanding. For the
original Twelve, this meant literal
suffering and death. For believers

today, it means understanding that we belong to Him and that we live to serve His purposes. Christians follow their Lord by imitating His life and obeying His commands. Following Christ in this life may be costly, but in the long run it is well worth the pain and effort.

"If you want to be my disciple, you must hate everyone else by comparison—your father and mother, wife and children, brothers and sisters— yes, even your own life. Otherwise, you cannot be my disciple. And if you do not carry your own cross and follow me, you cannot be my disciple."

LUKE 14:26-27

REFLECTION

Jesus' audience was well aware of what it meant to carry one's own cross. When the Romans led a criminal to his execution site, he was forced to carry the cross on which he would die. This showed his submission to Rome and warned observers that they had better submit too. Jesus made this statement to get the crowds to think through their enthusiasm for Him. He encouraged those who were superficial either to go deeper or to turn back. Following Christ means total submission to Him—perhaps even to the point of death.

"When a servant comes in from plowing or taking care of sheep, does his master say, 'Come in and eat with me'? No, he says, 'Prepare my meal, put on your apron, and serve me while I eat. Then you can eat later.' And does the master thank the servant for doing what he was told to do? Of course not. In the same way, when you obey me you should say, 'We are unworthy servants who have simply done our duty.'"

LUKE 17:7-10

REFLECTION

If we have obeyed God, we have only done our duty, and we should regard it as a privilege. Do you sometimes feel that you deserve extra credit for serving God? Remember, obedience is not something extra we do; it is our duty. Jesus is not suggesting that our service is meaningless or useless, nor is He advocating doing away with rewards. He is attacking unwarranted self-esteem and spiritual pride.

The Rewards of Following Jesus

"Everyone who has given up houses or brothers or sisters or father or mother or children or property, for my sake, will receive a hundred times as much in return and will inherit eternal life. But many who are the greatest now will be least important then, and those who seem least important now will be the greatest then."

MATTHEW 19:29-30

REFLECTION

Jesus turned the world's values upside down. Consider the most powerful or well-known people in our world—how many got where they are by being humble, self-effacing, and gentle? Not many! But in the life to come, the last will be first. Don't forfeit eternal rewards for temporary benefits. Be willing to make sacrifices now for greater rewards later. Be willing to accept human disapproval, while knowing that you have God's approval.

"I tell you the truth, everyone who acknowledges me publicly here on earth, the Son of Man will also acknowledge in the presence of God's angels."

LUKE 12:8

REFLECTION

We deny Jesus when we (1) hope no one will find out we are Christians, (2) decide *not* to speak up for what is right, (3) are silent about our relationship with God, (4) blend into society, and (5) accept our culture's non-Christian values. By contrast, we acknowledge Him when we (1) live moral, upright, Christ-honoring lives; (2) look for opportunities to share our faith with others; (3) help others in need; (4) take a stand for justice; (5) love others; (6) acknowledge our loyalty to Christ; and (7) use our lives and resources to carry out His desires rather than our own.

"My sheep listen to my voice; I know them, and they follow me. I give them eternal life, and they will never perish. No one can snatch them away from me, for my Father has given them to me, and he is more powerful than anyone else. No one can snatch them from the Father's hand."

JOHN 10:27-29

REFLECTION

Just as a shepherd protects his sheep, Jesus protects His people from eternal harm. While believers can expect to suffer on earth, Satan cannot harm their souls or take away their eternal life with God. There are many reasons to be afraid here on earth because this is the devil's domain. But if you choose to follow Jesus, He will give you everlasting safety.

The Authority of Jesus' Followers

"I tell you the truth, whatever you forbid on earth will be forbidden in heaven, and whatever you permit on earth will be permitted in heaven.

"I also tell you this: If two of you agree here on earth concerning anything you ask, my Father in heaven will do it for you. For where two or three gather together as my followers, I am there among them."

MATTHEW 18:18-20

REFLECTION

This *forbidding and permitting* refers to the decisions of the church in conflicts. Among believers, there should need to be no court of appeals beyond the church. Ideally, the church's decisions should be God-guided and based on discernment of His Word. Believers have the responsibility, therefore, to bring their problems to the church, and the church has the responsibility to use God's guidance in seeking to resolve conflicts. Handling problems God's way will have an impact now and for eternity.

"Go into all the world and preach the Good News to everyone. Anyone who believes and is baptized will be saved. But anyone who refuses to believe will be condemned."

MARK 16:15-16

REFLECTION

Jesus told His disciples to go into all the world, telling everyone that He had paid the penalty for sin and that those who believe in Him can be forgiven and live eternally with God. Christians today in all parts of the world are telling this Good News to people who haven't heard about Christ. The driving power that carries missionaries around the world and sets Christ's church in motion is the faith that comes from the Resurrection. Do you ever feel as though you don't have the skill or determination to be a witness for Christ? Press into your relationship with Christ. His Holy Spirit will lead you into opportunities and give you the wisdom to share His message.

"I tell you the truth, anyone who believes in me will do the same works I have done, and even greater works, because I am going to be with the Father. You can ask for anything in my name, and I will do it, so that the Son can bring glory to the Father."

JOHN 14:12-13

REFLECTION

Raising the dead is about as amazing as you can get; how could the disciples do greater things than that? The "even greater works" would come because the disciples, working in the power of the Holy Spirit, would carry the Good News of God's Kingdom out of Palestine and into the whole world.

"Yes, ask me for anything in my name, and I will do it!"

JOHN 14:14

REFLECTION

When Jesus says we can ask for anything, we must remember that our asking must be in His name—that is, according to God's character and will. God will not grant requests contrary to His nature or His will, and we cannot use His name as a magic formula to fulfill our selfish desires. If we are sincerely following God and seeking to do His will, then our requests will be in line with what He wants, and He will grant them.

The Mission of Jesus' Followers

"You are the salt of the earth. But what good is salt if it has lost its flavor? Can you make it salty again? It will be thrown out and trampled underfoot as worthless."

MATTHEW 5:13

REFLECTION

If a seasoning has no flavor, it has no value. If Christians make no effort to affect the world around them, they are of little value to God. If we are too much like the world, we are worthless.

Christians should not blend in with everyone else. Instead, we should affect others positively, just as seasoning brings out the best flavor in food.

"You are the light of the world—like a city on a hilltop that cannot be hidden. No one lights a lamp and then puts it under a basket. Instead, a lamp is placed on a stand, where it gives light to everyone in the house. In the same way, let your good deeds shine out for all to see, so that everyone will praise your heavenly Father."

MATTHEW 5:14-16

REFLECTION

If we live for Christ, we will glow like lights, showing others what Christ is like. Be a beacon of truth—don't shut your light off from the rest of the world.

"The harvest is great, but the workers are few. So pray to the Lord who is in charge of the harvest; ask him to send more workers into his fields."

MATTHEW 9:37-38

REFLECTION

Jesus looked at the crowds following Him and referred to them as a field ripe for harvest. Many people are ready to give their lives to Christ if someone would show them how. Jesus commands us to pray that people will respond to this need for workers. Often, when we pray for something, God answers our prayers by using *us*. Be prepared for God to use you to show another person the way to Him.

"Go and announce to them that the Kingdom of Heaven is near. Heal the sick, raise the dead, cure those with leprosy, and cast out demons. Give as freely as you have received!"

MATTHEW 10:7-8

REFLECTION

Jesus gave the disciples a principle to guide their actions as they ministered to others: "Give as freely as you have received!" Because God has showered us with His blessings, we should give generously to others of our time, love, and possessions.

"Look, I am sending you out as sheep among wolves. So be as shrewd as snakes and harmless as doves. But beware! For you will be handed over to the courts and will be flogged with whips in the synagogues. **You will stand trial before governors and kings because you are my followers. But this will be your opportunity to tell the rulers and other unbelievers about me."**

MATTHEW 10:16-18

REFLECTION

The opposition of the Pharisees would be like ravaging wolves. The disciples' only hope would be to look to their Shepherd for protection. We may face similar hostility. Like the disciples, we are not to be sheep-like in our attitude but sensible and prudent. We are not to be gullible pawns, but neither are we to be deceitful connivers. We must find a balance between wisdom and vulnerability to accomplish God's work.

"Go and make disciples of all the nations, baptizing them in the name of the Father and the Son and the Holy Spirit. Teach these new disciples to obey all the commands I have given you. And be sure of this: I am with you always, even to the end of the age."

MATTHEW 28:19-20

REFLECTION

Jesus' words affirm the reality of the Trinity. Some people accuse theologians of making up the concept of the Trinity and reading it into Scripture. As we see here, the concept comes directly from Jesus Himself. He did not instruct His followers to baptize in the *names* but in the *name* of the Father, Son, and Holy Spirit. The word *Trinity* does not occur in Scripture, but it well describes the three-in-one nature of the Father, Son, and Holy Spirit.

"You will receive power when the Holy Spirit comes upon you. And you will be my witnesses, telling people about me everywhere—in Jerusalem, throughout Judea, in Samaria, and to the ends of the earth."

ACTS 1:8

REFLECTION

The "power" believers receive from the Holy Spirit includes courage, boldness, confidence, insight, ability, and authority. The disciples would need all these gifts to fulfill their mission. If you believe in Jesus Christ, you can experience the power of the Holy Spirit in your life.

"The Good News about the Kingdom will be preached throughout the whole world, so that all nations will hear it; and then the end will come."

MATTHEW 24:14

REFLECTION

Jesus said that before He returns, the Good News about the Kingdom (the message of salvation) would be preached throughout the world. This was the disciples' mission—and it is ours today. Jesus talked about the end times and final judgment to show His followers the urgency of spreading the Good News of salvation to everyone.

Service and Leadership

"You know that the rulers in this world lord it over their people, and officials flaunt their authority over those under them. But among you it will be different. Whoever wants to be a leader among you must be your servant, and whoever wants to be first among you must become your slave. For even the Son of Man came not to be served but to serve others and to give his life as a ransom for many."

MATTHEW 20:25-28

REFLECTION

A real leader has a servant's heart. Servant leaders appreciate others' worth and realize that they're not above any job. If you see something that needs to be done, don't wait to be asked. Take the initiative and do it like a faithful servant.

"The greatest among you must be a servant. But those who exalt themselves will be humbled, and those who humble themselves will be exalted."

MATTHEW 23:11-12

REFLECTION

Jesus challenged society's norms. To Him, greatness comes from serving—giving of yourself to help God and others. Service keeps us aware of others' needs, and it stops us from focusing only on ourselves. Jesus came as a servant. What kind of greatness do you seek?

After they arrived at Capernaum and settled in a house, Jesus asked his disciples, "What were you discussing out on the road?" But they didn't answer, because they had been arguing about which of them was the greatest. He sat down, called the twelve disciples over to him, and said, "Whoever wants to be first must take last place and be the servant of everyone else."

MARK 9:33-35

REFLECTION

Jesus described leadership from a new perspective. Serving others is real leadership. Instead of *using* people, we are to *serve* them. Jesus' mission was to serve others and to give His life away.

After washing their feet, he put on his robe again and sat down and asked, "Do you understand what I was doing? You call me 'Teacher' and 'Lord,' and you are right, because that's what I am. And since I, your Lord and Teacher, have washed your feet, you ought to wash each other's feet. I have given you an example to follow. Do as I have done to you."

JOHN 13:12-15

REFLECTION

Jesus did not wash His disciples' feet just to get them to be nice to each other. His far greater goal was to extend His mission on earth after He was gone. These men were to move into the world serving God, serving each other, and serving all people to whom they took the message of salvation.

PROMISES
OF JESUS

Comfort, Peace, and Rest

"Come to me, all of you who are
weary and carry heavy burdens, and I
will give you rest. Take my yoke upon
you. Let me teach you, because I am
humble and gentle at heart, and you
will find rest for your souls. For my
yoke is easy to bear, and the burden
I give you is light."

MATTHEW 11:28-30

REFLECTION

A person may be carrying heavy
burdens of (1) sin, (2) exces-
sive demands of religious leaders,
(3) oppression and persecution,
or (4) weariness in the search for

God. Jesus frees people from all these burdens. The rest that Jesus promises is love, healing, and peace with God, not the end of all labor. A relationship with God changes meaningless, wearisome toil into spiritual productivity and purpose.

"I tell you not to worry about everyday life—whether you have enough food to eat or enough clothes to wear. For life is more than food, and your body more than clothing. Look at the ravens. They don't plant or harvest or store food in barns, for God feeds them. And you are far more valuable to him than any birds! Can all your worries add a single moment to your life? And if worry can't accomplish a little thing like that, what's the use of worrying over bigger things?

"Look at the lilies and how they grow. They don't work or make their

clothing, yet Solomon in all his glory
was not dressed as beautifully as they
are. And if God cares so wonderfully
for flowers that are here today and
thrown into the fire tomorrow, he will
certainly care for you. Why do you
have so little faith?"

LUKE 12:22-28

REFLECTION

Jesus commands us not to worry.
But how can we avoid it? Only faith
can free us from the anxiety caused
by greed and covetousness. Working
and planning responsibly is good;
dwelling on all the ways our planning could go wrong is bad. Worry
is pointless because it can't fill any of
our needs; worry is foolish because
the Creator of the universe loves
us and knows what we need. He
promises to meet all our real needs
but not necessarily all our desires.

"I am leaving you with a gift—peace of mind and heart. And the peace I give is a gift the world cannot give. So don't be troubled or afraid. Remember what I told you: I am going away, but I will come back to you again. If you really loved me, you would be happy that I am going to the Father, who is greater than I am."

JOHN 14:27-28

REFLECTION

Sin, fear, uncertainty, doubt, and numerous other forces are at war within us. The peace of God moves into our hearts and lives to restrain these hostile forces and offer comfort in place of conflict. Jesus says He will give us that peace if we are willing to accept it from Him.

The Hope of Heaven

"Don't let your hearts be troubled. Trust in God, and trust also in me. There is more than enough room in my Father's home. If this were not so, would I have told you that I am going to prepare a place for you? When everything is ready, I will come and get you, so that you will always be with me where I am. And you know the way to where I am going."

JOHN 14:1-4

REFLECTION

Jesus' words show that the way to eternal life, though unseen, is secure—as secure as your trust in Jesus. He has already prepared the way to eternal life. The only issue that may still be unsettled is your willingness to believe.

The Holy Spirit

"I will ask the Father, and he will give you another Advocate, who will never leave you. He is the Holy Spirit, who leads into all truth. The world cannot receive him, because it isn't looking for him and doesn't recognize him. But you know him, because he lives with you now and later will be in you. No, I will not abandon you as orphans—I will come to you. Soon the world will no longer see me, but you will see me. Since I live, you also will live."

JOHN 14:16-19

REFLECTION

Jesus was soon going to leave the disciples, but He would remain with them. How could this be? The Advocate—the Spirit of God Himself—would come after Jesus was gone to care for and guide the disciples. The Holy Spirit is the very presence of God within us and all believers, helping us live as God wants and building Christ's church on earth. By faith we can appropriate the Spirit's power each day.

"**When the Father sends the Advocate as my representative—that is, the Holy Spirit—he will teach you everything and will remind you of everything I have told you.**"

JOHN 14:26

REFLECTION

Jesus promised the disciples that the Holy Spirit would help them remember what He had been teaching them. This promise ensures the validity of the New Testament. The disciples were eyewitnesses of Jesus' life and teachings, and the Holy Spirit helped them remember without taking away their individual perspectives. The Holy Spirit can help us in the same way. As we study the Bible, we can trust Him to plant truth in our minds, convince us of God's will, and remind us when we stray from it.

"I will send you the Advocate—the Spirit of truth. He will come to you from the Father and will testify all about me."

JOHN 15:26

REFLECTION

Once again Jesus offers hope. The Holy Spirit gives strength to endure the unreasonable hatred and evil in our world and the hostility many have toward Christ. This is especially comforting for those facing persecution.

"In fact, it is best for you that I go away, because if I don't, the Advocate won't come. If I do go away, then I will send him to you. And when he comes, he will convict the world of its sin, and of God's righteousness, and of the coming judgment."

JOHN 16:7-8

REFLECTION

Unless Jesus did what He came to do, there would be no Good News. If He did not die, He could not remove our sins; He could not rise again and defeat death. If He did not go back to the Father, the Holy Spirit would not come. Christ's presence on earth was limited to one place at a time. His leaving meant He could be present to the whole world through the Holy Spirit.

"When the Spirit of truth comes, he will guide you into all truth. He will not speak on his own but will tell you what he has heard. He will tell you about the future. He will bring me glory by telling you whatever he receives from me. All that belongs to the Father is mine; this is why I said, 'The Spirit will tell you whatever he receives from me.'"

JOHN 16:13-15

REFLECTION

The truth into which the Holy
Spirit guides us is the truth about
Christ. The Spirit also helps us
through patient practice to discern right from wrong.

The Return of Jesus

"At last, the sign that the Son of Man is coming will appear in the heavens, and there will be deep mourning among all the peoples of the earth. And they will see the Son of Man coming on the clouds of heaven with power and great glory. And he will send out his angels with the mighty blast of a trumpet, and they will gather his chosen ones from all over the world—from the farthest ends of the earth and heaven."

MATTHEW 24:30-31

REFLECTION

The nations of the earth will mourn because unbelievers will suddenly realize they have chosen the wrong side. Everything they have scoffed about will be happening, and it will be too late for them.

"Heaven and earth will disappear, but my words will never disappear.

"However, no one knows the day or hour when these things will happen, not even the angels in heaven or the Son himself. Only the Father knows.

"When the Son of Man returns, it will be like it was in Noah's day. In those days before the flood, the people were enjoying banquets and parties and weddings right up to the time Noah entered his boat. People didn't realize what was going to happen until the flood came and swept them all away. That is the way it will be when the Son of Man comes.

"Two men will be working together in the field; one will be taken, the other left. Two women will be grinding flour at the mill; one will be taken, the other left.

"So you, too, must keep watch! For you don't know what day your Lord is coming. Understand this: If a homeowner knew exactly when a burglar was coming, he would keep watch and not permit his house to be broken into. You also must be ready all the time, for the Son of Man will come when least expected."

MATTHEW 24:35-44

REFLECTION

It is good that we don't know exactly when Christ will return. If we knew the precise date, we might be tempted to be lazy in our work for Christ. Worse yet, we might plan to keep sinning and then turn to God right at the end. Heaven is not our only goal; we have work to do here. And we must keep on doing it until death or until we see the unmistakable return of our Savior.

"Be dressed for service and keep your lamps burning, as though you were waiting for your master to return from the wedding feast. Then you will be ready to open the door and let him in the moment he arrives and knocks. The servants who are ready and waiting for his return will be rewarded. I tell you the truth, he himself will seat them, put on an apron, and serve them as they sit and eat! He may come in the middle of the night or just before dawn. But whenever he comes, he will reward the servants who are ready.

"Understand this: If a homeowner knew exactly when a burglar was coming, he would not permit his house to be broken into. You also must be ready all the time, for the Son of Man will come when least expected."

LUKE 12:35-40

REFLECTION

Jesus repeatedly said that He would leave this world but would return at some future time. He also said that a Kingdom was being prepared for His followers.

Many Greeks envisioned this as a heavenly, idealized, spiritual Kingdom. Jews—like Isaiah and John, the writer of Revelation—saw it as a restored earthly Kingdom.

"Look, I am coming soon, bringing my reward with me to repay all people according to their deeds. I am the Alpha and the Omega, the First and the Last, the Beginning and the End. . . . I, Jesus, have sent my angel to give you this message for the churches. I am both the source of David and the heir to his throne. I am the bright morning star."

REVELATION 22:12-13, 16

REFLECTION

Jesus is both David's "source" and "heir." As the Creator of all, Jesus existed long before David. As a human, however, He was one of David's direct descendants. As the Messiah, He is the "bright morning star," the light of salvation to all.

LOVE

God's Love

"This is how God loved the world:
He gave his one and only Son, so that
everyone who believes in him will
not perish but have eternal life. God
sent his Son into the world not to
judge the world, but to save the world
through him."

JOHN 3:16-17

REFLECTION

The message of the Good News
comes to a focus in this verse.
God's love is not static or self-
centered; it reaches out and draws
others in. Here God sets the

pattern of true love, the basis for all love relationships—when you love someone dearly, you are willing to give freely to the point of self-sacrifice. God paid dearly with the life of His Son, the highest price He could pay. Jesus accepted our punishment, paid the price for our sins, and then offered us the new life that He had bought for us. When we share the Good News with others, our love must be like Jesus'—willingly giving up our own comfort and security so that others might join us in receiving God's love.

"I have loved you even as the Father has loved me. Remain in my love. When you obey my commandments, you remain in my love, just as I obey my Father's commandments

and remain in his love. I have told
you these things so that you will be
filled with my joy. Yes, your joy will
overflow!"

JOHN 15:9-11

REFLECTION

When things are going well,
we feel elated. When hardships
come, we sink into depression.
But true joy transcends the roll-
ing waves of circumstance. Joy
comes from a consistent relationship with Jesus Christ. When our
lives are intertwined with His,
He will help us walk through
adversity without sinking into
debilitating lows and manage
prosperity without moving into
deceptive highs. The joy of living
with Jesus Christ daily will keep
us levelheaded, no matter how
high or low our circumstances.

"Even the Son of Man came not to be served but to serve others and to give his life as a ransom for many."

MARK 10:45

REFLECTION

This verse reveals not only the motive for Jesus' ministry but also the basis for our salvation. A ransom was the price paid to release a slave. Jesus paid a ransom for us because we could not pay it ourselves. His death released all of us from our slavery to sin. The disciples thought Jesus' life and power would save them from Rome; Jesus said His *death* would save them from sin, an even greater slavery than Rome's.

Loving God

"Those who accept my commandments and obey them are the ones who love me. And because they love me, my Father will love them. And I will love them and reveal myself to each of them."

JOHN 14:21

REFLECTION

Jesus said that His followers show their love for Him by obeying Him. Love is more than lovely words; it is commitment and conduct. If you love Christ, then prove it by obeying what He says in His Word.

"If you love your father or mother more than you love me, you are not worthy of being mine; or if you love your son or daughter more than me, you are not worthy of being mine."

MATTHEW 10:37

REFLECTION

Christ calls us to a higher mission than to find comfort and tranquillity in this life. Love of family is a law of God, but even this love can be self-serving and used as an excuse not to serve God or do His work.

"'You must love the LORD your God with all your heart, all your soul, and all your mind.' This is the first and greatest commandment. A second is equally important: 'Love your neighbor as yourself.'

The entire law and all the demands of the prophets are based on these two commandments."

MATTHEW 22:37-40

REFLECTION

The Pharisees, who had classified over six hundred laws, often tried to distinguish the more important from the less important. So one of them, an expert in religious law, asked Jesus to identify the most important law. Jesus quoted from Deuteronomy 6:5 and Leviticus 19:18. By fulfilling these two commands, a person keeps all the others. They summarize the Ten Commandments and the other Old Testament moral laws.

"Look at this woman kneeling here. When I entered your home, you didn't offer me water to wash the dust from my feet, but she has washed them with her tears and wiped them with her hair. You didn't greet me with a kiss, but from the time I first came in, she has not stopped kissing my feet. You neglected the courtesy of olive oil to anoint my head, but she has anointed my feet with rare perfume.

"I tell you, her sins—and they are many—have been forgiven, so she has shown me much love. But a person who is forgiven little shows only little love."

LUKE 7:44-47

REFLECTION

Overflowing love is the natural response to forgiveness and the appropriate consequence of faith.

But only those who realize the depth of their sin can appreciate the complete forgiveness that God offers them. Jesus has rescued all of His followers, whether they were once extremely wicked or conventionally good, from eternal death. Do you appreciate the wideness of God's mercy? Are you grateful for His forgiveness?

Loving Others

"I am giving you a new commandment: Love each other. Just as I have loved you, you should love each other. Your love for one another will prove to the world that you are my disciples."

JOHN 13:34-35

REFLECTION

Jesus says that our Christlike love will show we are His disciples. Do people see petty bickering, jealousy, and division in your church? Or do they know you are Jesus' followers by your love for one another?

"This is my commandment: Love each other in the same way I have loved you. There is no greater love than to lay down one's life for one's friends. You are my friends if you do what I command."

JOHN 15:12-14

REFLECTION

We are to love each other as Jesus loved us, and He loved us enough to give His life for us. We may not have to die for someone, but there are other ways to practice sacrificial love: listening, helping, encouraging, giving. Think of someone in particular who needs this kind of love today. Give all the love you can, and then try to give a little more.

"You have heard the law that says, 'Love your neighbor' and hate your enemy. But I say, love your enemies! Pray for those who persecute you! In that way, you will be acting as true children of your Father in heaven. For he gives his sunlight to both the evil and the good, and he sends rain on the just and the unjust alike."

MATTHEW 5:43-45

REFLECTION
> By telling us not to retaliate,
> Jesus keeps us from taking
> the law into our own hands.
> By loving and praying for our
> enemies, we can overcome evil
> with good.

"To you who are willing to listen, I say, love your enemies! Do good to those who hate you. Bless those who curse you. Pray for those who hurt you. If someone slaps you on one cheek, offer the other cheek also. If someone demands your coat, offer your shirt also. Give to anyone who asks; and when things are taken away from you, don't try to get them back. Do to others as you would like them to do to you."

LUKE 6:27-31

REFLECTION

The Jews despised the Romans because they oppressed God's people, but Jesus told the people to love these enemies. Such words turned many away from Christ. Jesus wasn't talking about having affection for enemies; He was talking about an act of the will. You can't "fall into" this kind of love— it takes conscious effort. Loving our enemies means acting in their best interests. We can pray for them, and we can think of ways to help them. Jesus loves the whole world, even though the world is in rebellion against God. Jesus asks us to follow His example by loving our enemies. Grant your enemies the same respect and rights as you desire for yourself.

"If you love only those who love you, why should you get credit for that? Even sinners love those who love them! And if you do good only to those who do good to you, why should you get credit? Even sinners do that much! And if you lend money only to those who can repay you, why should you get credit? Even sinners will lend to other sinners for a full return."

LUKE 6:32-34

REFLECTION

Love means action. One way to put love to work is to take the initiative in meeting specific needs. This is easy to do with people who love us, people whom we trust; but love means doing this even to those who may not like us or can hurt us. The money we give others should be a gift, not a high-interest loan that will put a burden on them. Give as though you are giving to God.

"A Jewish man was traveling from Jerusalem down to Jericho, and he was attacked by bandits. They stripped him of his clothes, beat him up, and left him half dead beside the road.

"By chance a priest came along. But when he saw the man lying there, he crossed to the other side of the road and passed him by. A Temple assistant walked over and looked at him lying there, but he also passed by on the other side.

"Then a despised Samaritan came along, and when he saw the man, he felt compassion for him. Going over to him, the Samaritan soothed his wounds with olive oil and wine and bandaged them. Then he put the man on his own donkey and took him to an inn, where he took care of him. The next day he handed the innkeeper two silver coins, telling him, 'Take care of this man. If his bill runs higher than this, I'll pay you the next time I'm here.'

"Now which of these three would you say was a neighbor to the man who was attacked by bandits?" Jesus asked.

The man replied, "The one who showed him mercy."

Then Jesus said, "Yes, now go and do the same."

LUKE 10:30-37

REFLECTION

A deep hatred existed between Jews and Samaritans. The Jews saw themselves as pure descendants of Abraham, while the Samaritans were a mixed race produced when Jews from the northern kingdom intermarried with other peoples after Israel's exile. To this legal expert, the person least likely to act correctly would be the Samaritan. In fact, he did not even say the word *Samaritan* in answer to Jesus' question. This expert's attitude betrayed his lack of the very thing that he had earlier said the law commanded—love.

FORGIVENESS

FORGIVENESS

God's Forgiveness

"If a man has a hundred sheep and one of them wanders away, what will he do? Won't he leave the ninety-nine others on the hills and go out to search for the one that is lost? And if he finds it, I tell you the truth, he will rejoice over it more than over the ninety-nine that didn't wander away! In the same way, it is not my heavenly Father's will that even one of these little ones should perish."

MATTHEW 18:12-14

REFLECTION

Just as a shepherd is concerned
enough about one lost sheep to
go search the hills for it, so God
is concerned about every human
being He has created. If you
come in contact with children
in your neighborhood who need
Christ, steer them toward Him
by your example, your words,
and your acts of kindness.

"Suppose a woman has ten silver
coins and loses one. Won't she light
a lamp and sweep the entire house
and search carefully until she finds
it? And when she finds it, she will
call in her friends and neighbors and
say, 'Rejoice with me because I have
found my lost coin.' In the same way,
there is joy in the presence of God's
angels when even one sinner repents."

LUKE 15:8-10

REFLECTION

Palestinian women received ten silver coins as a wedding gift. Besides their monetary value, these coins held sentimental value like that of a wedding ring, and to lose one would be extremely distressing. Just as a woman would rejoice at finding her lost coin, so the angels rejoice over a repentant sinner. Each individual is precious to God. He grieves over every loss and rejoices whenever one of His children is found and brought into the Kingdom. Perhaps we would have more joy in our churches if we shared Jesus' love and concern for the lost.

"A man had two sons. The younger son told his father, 'I want my share of your estate now before you die.' So his father agreed to divide his wealth between his sons.

"A few days later this younger son packed all his belongings and moved to a distant land, and there he wasted all his money in wild living. About the time his money ran out, a great famine swept over the land, and he began to starve. He persuaded a local farmer to hire him, and the man sent him into his fields to feed the pigs. The young man became so hungry that even the pods he was feeding the pigs looked good to him. But no one gave him anything.

"When he finally came to his senses, he said to himself, 'At home even the hired servants have food enough to spare, and here I am dying of hunger!

I will go home to my father and say, "Father, I have sinned against both heaven and you, and I am no longer worthy of being called your son. Please take me on as a hired servant."'

"So he returned home to his father. And while he was still a long way off, his father saw him coming. Filled with love and compassion, he ran to his son, embraced him, and kissed him. His son said to him, 'Father, I have sinned against both heaven and you, and I am no longer worthy of being called your son.'

"But his father said to the servants, 'Quick! Bring the finest robe in the house and put it on him. Get a ring for his finger and sandals for his feet. And kill the calf we have been fattening. We must celebrate with a feast, for this son of mine was dead and has now returned to life. He was lost, but now he is found.' So the party began.

"Meanwhile, the older son was in the fields working. When he returned home, he heard music and dancing in the house, and he asked one of the servants what was going on. 'Your brother is back,' he was told, 'and your father has killed the fattened calf. We are celebrating because of his safe return.'

"The older brother was angry and wouldn't go in. His father came out and begged him, but he replied, 'All these years I've slaved for you and never once refused to do a single thing you told me to. And in all that time you never gave me even one young goat for a feast with my friends. Yet when this son of yours comes back after squandering your money on prostitutes, you celebrate by killing the fattened calf!'

"His father said to him, 'Look,
dear son, you have always stayed by
me, and everything I have is yours.
We had to celebrate this happy day.
For your brother was dead and has
come back to life! He was lost, but
now he is found!'"

LUKE 15:11-32

REFLECTION

In this story, the father watched
and waited. He was dealing with
a human being with a will of his
own, but he was ready to greet
his son if he returned. In the
same way, God's love is constant
and patient and welcoming. He
will search for us and give us
opportunities to respond, but He
will not force us to come to Him.
Like the father in this story, God
waits patiently for us to come to
our senses.

Forgiving Others

"If you forgive those who sin against you, your heavenly Father will forgive you. But if you refuse to forgive others, your Father will not forgive your sins."

MATTHEW 6:14-15

REFLECTION

Jesus gives a startling warning about forgiveness: if we refuse to forgive others, God will also refuse to forgive us. Why? Because when we don't forgive others, we are denying our common ground as sinners in need of God's forgiveness. God's forgiveness of sin is not the direct result of our forgiving others, but it is based on our realizing what forgiveness means. It is easy to ask God for forgiveness but difficult to grant it to others. Whenever we ask God to forgive us for sin, we should ask, Have I forgiven the people who have wronged me?

"The Kingdom of Heaven can be compared to a king who decided to bring his accounts up to date with servants who had borrowed money from him. In the process, one of his debtors was brought in who owed him millions of dollars. He couldn't pay, so his master ordered that he be sold—along with his wife, his children, and everything he owned—to pay the debt.

"But the man fell down before

his master and begged him, 'Please, be patient with me, and I will pay it all.' Then his master was filled with pity for him, and he released him and forgave his debt.

"But when the man left the king, he went to a fellow servant who owed him a few thousand dollars. He grabbed him by the throat and demanded instant payment.

"His fellow servant fell down before him and begged for a little more time. 'Be patient with me, and I will pay it,' he pleaded. But his creditor wouldn't wait. He had the man arrested and put in prison until the debt could be paid in full.

"When some of the other servants saw this, they were very upset. They went to the king and told him everything that had happened. Then the king called in the man he had

forgiven and said, 'You evil servant!
I forgave you that tremendous
debt because you pleaded with me.
Shouldn't you have mercy on your
fellow servant, just as I had mercy on
you?' Then the angry king sent the
man to prison to be tortured until he
had paid his entire debt.

"That's what my heavenly Father will
do to you if you refuse to forgive your
brothers and sisters from your heart."

MATTHEW 18:23-35

REFLECTION

Because God has forgiven all our
sins, we should not withhold
forgiveness from others. As we
realize how completely Christ has
forgiven us, it should produce
an attitude of forgiveness toward
others. When we don't forgive
others, we are setting ourselves
above Christ's law of love.

PRAYER

PRAYER

Learning to Pray

Pray like this:

"Our Father in heaven,
may your name be kept holy.
May your Kingdom come soon.
May your will be done on earth,
as it is in heaven.
Give us today the food we need,
and forgive us our sins,
as we have forgiven those who
sin against us.
And don't let us yield to temptation,
but rescue us from the evil one."

MATTHEW 6:9-13

REFLECTION

This is often called the Lord's Prayer because Jesus gave it to the disciples as a model for them (and us) to keep in mind as we pray. It can be a pattern for our prayers. We should praise God, pray for His work in the world, pray for our daily needs, and pray for help in our daily struggles.

"When you pray, don't be like the hypocrites who love to pray publicly on street corners and in the synagogues where everyone can see them. I tell you the truth, that is all the reward they will ever get. But when you pray, go away by yourself, shut the door behind you, and pray to your Father in private. Then your Father, who sees everything, will reward you."

MATTHEW 6:5-6

REFLECTION

Some people, especially the religious leaders, wanted to be seen as "holy," and public prayer was one way to get attention. Jesus saw through their self-righteous acts, however, and taught that the essence of prayer is not public style but private communication with God. There is a place for public prayer, but to pray only where others will notice you indicates that your real audience is not God.

"Two men went to the Temple to pray. One was a Pharisee, and the other was a despised tax collector. The Pharisee stood by himself and prayed this prayer: 'I thank you, God, that I am not a sinner like everyone else. For I don't cheat, I don't sin, and I don't commit adultery. I'm certainly not like that tax collector! I fast twice a week, and I give you a tenth of my income.'

"But the tax collector stood at a distance and dared not even lift his eyes to heaven as he prayed. Instead, he beat his chest in sorrow, saying, 'O God, be merciful to me, for I am a sinner.' I tell you, this sinner, not the Pharisee, returned home justified before God. For those who exalt themselves will be humbled, and those who humble themselves will be exalted."

LUKE 18:10-14

REFLECTION

The Pharisee did not go to the Temple to pray to God but to announce to all within earshot how good he was. The tax collector went recognizing his sin and begging for mercy. Self-righteousness is dangerous. It leads to pride, causes a person to despise others, and prevents him or her from learning anything from God. The tax collector's prayer should be our prayer because we all need God's mercy every day. Don't let pride in your achievements cut you off from God.

"When you pray, don't babble on and on as people of other religions do. They think their prayers are answered merely by repeating their words again and again. Don't be like them, for your Father knows exactly what you need even before you ask him!"

MATTHEW 6:7-8

REFLECTION

Repeating the same words over and over like a magic incantation is no way to ensure that God will hear your prayer. It's not wrong to come to God many times with the same requests—Jesus encourages *persistent* prayer. But He condemns the shallow repetition of words that are not offered with a sincere heart. We can never pray too much if our prayers are honest and sincere. Before you start to pray, make sure you mean what you say.

Persistence in Prayer

"Keep on asking, and you will receive what you ask for. Keep on seeking, and you will find. Keep on knocking, and the door will be opened to you. For everyone who asks, receives. Everyone who seeks, finds. And to everyone who knocks, the door will be opened.

"You parents—if your children ask for a loaf of bread, do you give them a stone instead? Or if they ask for a fish, do you give them a snake? Of course not! So if you sinful people know how to give good gifts to your children, how much more will your heavenly Father give good gifts to those who ask him."

MATTHEW 7:7-11

REFLECTION

Jesus tells us to persist in pursuing God. People often give up after a few halfhearted efforts and conclude that God cannot be found. But knowing God takes faith, focus, and follow-through, and Jesus assures us that we will be rewarded. Don't give up in your efforts to seek God. Continue to ask Him for more knowledge, patience, wisdom, love, and understanding. He will give them to you.

"Suppose you went to a friend's house at midnight, wanting to borrow three loaves of bread. You say to him, 'A friend of mine has just arrived for a visit, and I have nothing for him to eat.' And suppose he calls out from his bedroom, 'Don't bother me. The door is locked for the night, and my family and I are all in bed. I can't help you.' But I tell you this—though he won't do it for friendship's sake, if you keep knocking long enough, he will get up and give you whatever you need because of your shameless persistence.

"And so I tell you, keep on asking, and you will receive what you ask for. Keep on seeking, and you will find. Keep on knocking, and the door will be opened to you. For everyone who asks, receives. Everyone who seeks, finds. And to everyone who knocks, the door will be opened."

LUKE 11:5-10

REFLECTION

Persistence, or boldness, in prayer overcomes *our* insensitivity, not God's. To practice persistence does more to change our hearts and minds than His, and it helps us understand and express the intensity of our need. Persistence in prayer helps us recognize God's work.

"There was a judge in a certain city," [Jesus] said, "who neither feared God nor cared about people. A widow of that city came to him repeatedly, saying, 'Give me justice in this dispute with my enemy.' The judge ignored her for a while, but finally he said to himself, 'I don't fear God or care about people, but this woman is driving me crazy. I'm going to see that she gets justice,

because she is wearing me out with
her constant requests!'"

Luke 18:2-5

Reflection

If godless judges respond to
constant pressure, how much
more will a great and loving God
respond to us? If we know He
loves us, we can believe He will
hear our cries for help.

The Results of Prayer

"You will ask in my name. I'm not saying I will ask the Father on your behalf, for the Father himself loves you dearly because you love me and believe that I came from God."

<small>JOHN 16:26-27</small>

REFLECTION

Jesus is talking about a new relationship between the believer and God. Previously, people approached God through priests. After Jesus' resurrection, any believer could approach God directly. A new day has dawned and now all believers are priests, talking with God personally and directly. We approach God, not because of our own merit, but because Jesus, our great High Priest, has made us acceptable to God.

"You fathers—if your children ask for a fish, do you give them a snake instead? Or if they ask for an egg, do you give them a scorpion? Of course not! So if you sinful people know how to give good gifts to your children, how much more will your heavenly Father give the Holy Spirit to those who ask him."

LUKE 11:11-13

REFLECTION

Even though good fathers make mistakes, they treat their children well. How much better our perfect heavenly Father treats His children! The most important gift He could ever give us is the Holy Spirit, whom He promised to give all believers after [Jesus'] death, resurrection, and return to heaven.

The Importance of Faith

"I tell you the truth, if you have faith and don't doubt, you can do things like this and much more. You can even say to this mountain, 'May you be lifted up and thrown into the sea,' and it will happen. You can pray for anything, and if you have faith, you will receive it."

MATTHEW 21:21-22

REFLECTION

Many have wondered about Jesus' statement that if we have faith and don't doubt, we can move mountains. Jesus,

of course, was not suggesting
that His followers use prayer
as "magic" and perform capri-
cious, "mountain-moving"
acts. Instead, He was making
a strong point about the disciples' (and our) lack of faith.
What kinds of mountains do
you face? Have you talked to
God about them? How strong is
your faith?

**"Have faith in God. I tell you the
truth, you can say to this mountain,
'May you be lifted up and thrown
into the sea,' and it will happen. But
you must really believe it will happen
and have no doubt in your heart. I
tell you, you can pray for anything,
and if you believe that you've received
it, it will be yours. But when you are
praying, first forgive anyone you are**

holding a grudge against, so that your
Father in heaven will forgive your
sins, too."

MARK 11:22-25

REFLECTION

Jesus, our example, prayed,
"Everything is possible for
you. . . . Yet I want your will
to be done, not mine" (Mark
14:36). Our prayers are often
motivated by our own interests
and desires. We like to hear
that we can have anything. But
Jesus prayed with *God*'s interests in mind. When we pray, we
can express our desires, but we
should want His will above ours.
Check yourself to see if your
prayers focus on your interests
or God's.

Prayers of Jesus

This is how you should pray:

"Father, may your name be kept
holy.
May your Kingdom come soon.
Give us each day the food we need,
and forgive us our sins,
as we forgive those who sin
against us.
And don't let us yield to temptation."

Luke 11:2-4

REFLECTION

Notice the order in this prayer. First, Jesus praised God; then He made His requests. Praising God first puts us in the right frame of mind to tell Him about our needs. Too often our prayers are more like shopping lists than conversations. These verses focus on three aspects of prayer: its content, our persistence, and God's faithfulness.

"Father, the hour has come. Glorify your Son so he can give glory back to you. For you have given him authority over everyone. He gives eternal life to each one you have given him. And this is the way to have eternal life—to know you, the only true God, and Jesus Christ, the one you sent to earth. I brought glory to you here on earth by completing the work you gave me to do. Now, Father, bring me into the glory we shared before the world began.

"I have revealed you to the ones you gave me from this world. They were always yours. You gave them to me, and they have kept your word. Now they know that everything I have is a gift from you, for I have passed on to them the message you gave me. They accepted it and know that I came from you, and they believe you sent me.

"My prayer is not for the world, but for those you have given me, because they belong to you. All who are mine belong to you, and you have given them to me, so they bring me glory. Now I am departing from the world; they are staying in this world, but I am coming to you. Holy Father,

you have given me your name; now
protect them by the power of your
name so that they will be united just
as we are. During my time here, I
protected them by the power of the
name you gave me. I guarded them
so that not one was lost, except the
one headed for destruction, as the
Scriptures foretold.

"Now I am coming to you. I told
them many things while I was with
them in this world so they would be
filled with my joy. I have given them
your word. And the world hates them
because they do not belong to the
world, just as I do not belong to the
world. I'm not asking you to take
them out of the world, but to keep
them safe from the evil one. They
do not belong to this world any more
than I do. Make them holy by your
truth; teach them your word, which

is truth. Just as you sent me into the world, I am sending them into the world. And I give myself as a holy sacrifice for them so they can be made holy by your truth.

"I am praying not only for these disciples but also for all who will ever believe in me through their message. I pray that they will all be one, just as you and I are one—as you are in me, Father, and I am in you. And may they be in us so that the world will believe you sent me.

"I have given them the glory you gave me, so they may be one as we are one. I am in them and you are in me. May they experience such perfect unity that the world will know that you sent me and that you love them as much as you love me. Father, I want these whom you have given me to be with me where I am. Then they can see all the glory you gave me because you loved me even before the world began!

"O righteous Father, the world doesn't know you, but I do; and these disciples know you sent me. I have revealed you to them, and I will continue to do so. Then your love for me will be in them, and I will be in them."

JOHN 17:1-26

REFLECTION

From Jesus' prayer we learn that the world is a tremendous battleground where the forces under Satan's power and those under God's authority are at war. Satan and his forces are motivated by bitter hatred for Christ and His forces. Jesus prayed for His disciples, including those of us who follow Him today. He prayed

that God would keep His chosen
believers safe from Satan's power,
setting them apart and making them pure and holy, uniting
them through His truth.

**"My Father! If it is possible, let this
cup of suffering be taken away from
me. Yet I want your will to be done,
not mine. . . . My Father! If this cup
cannot be taken away unless I drink
it, your will be done."**

MATTHEW 26:39, 42

REFLECTION

Jesus was not rebelling against His
Father's will when He asked that
the cup of suffering and separation be taken away. In fact, He
reaffirmed His desire to do God's
will by saying, "Yet I want your
will to be done, not mine." His
prayer reveals to us His terrible

suffering. His agony was worse than death because He paid for *all* sin by being separated from God. The sinless Son of God took our sins upon Himself to save us from suffering and separation.

"Eli, Eli, lema sabachthani? . . . My God, my God, why have you abandoned me?"

MATTHEW 27:46

REFLECTION

Jesus was not questioning God; He was quoting the first line of Psalm 22—a deep expression of the anguish He felt when He took on the sins of the world, which caused Him to be separated from His Father. *This* was what Jesus dreaded as He prayed to God in the garden to take the cup from Him. The physical agony was horrible, but even worse was the period of spiritual separation from God. Jesus suffered this double death so that we would never have to experience eternal separation from God.

"Father, forgive them, for they don't know what they are doing."
LUKE 23:34

REFLECTION

Jesus asked God to forgive the people who were putting Him to death—Jewish leaders, Roman politicians and soldiers, bystanders—and God answered that prayer by opening up the way of salvation even to Jesus' murderers. Jesus was suffering the most horrible, painful death ever devised by sinful man, and He looked at the people responsible for His suffering and prayed for their forgiveness. Because we are all sinners, we all played a part in putting Jesus to death. The Good News is that God is gracious. He will forgive us and give us new life through His Son.

"Father, I entrust my spirit into your hands!"

LUKE 23:46

REFLECTION

It is believed that this prayer, Jesus' final words on the cross, is part of David's Psalm 31. Regardless of what is going on in our lives, we need to entrust ourselves into our Father's hands.

THE KINGDOM
OF GOD

The Nature of the Kingdom

"The Kingdom of Heaven is like
a mustard seed planted in a field.
It is the smallest of all seeds, but it
becomes the largest of garden plants;
it grows into a tree, and birds come
and make nests in its branches."

MATTHEW 13:31-32

REFLECTION

The mustard seed was the smallest seed a farmer used. Jesus used
this parable to show that the
Kingdom has small beginnings
but will grow and produce great
results.

"The Kingdom of Heaven is like the yeast a woman used in making bread. Even though she put only a little yeast in three measures of flour, it permeated every part of the dough."

MATTHEW 13:33

REFLECTION

In other Bible passages, yeast is used as a symbol of evil or uncleanness. Here it is a positive symbol of growth. Although yeast looks like a minor ingredient, it permeates the whole loaf. The Kingdom began small and was nearly invisible, but it would soon grow and have a great impact on the world.

"The Kingdom of Heaven is like a treasure that a man discovered hidden in a field. In his excitement, he hid it again and sold everything he owned to get enough money to buy the field."

MATTHEW 13:44

REFLECTION

The Kingdom of Heaven is more valuable than anything else we can have, and a person must be willing to give up everything to obtain it. The man who discovered the treasure hidden in the field stumbled upon it by accident but knew its value when he found it. Although the transaction cost the man everything, he paid nothing for the priceless treasure itself. It came free, with the field. Nothing is more precious than the Kingdom of Heaven; yet God gives it to us as a gift.

"The Kingdom of Heaven is like a merchant on the lookout for choice pearls. When he discovered a pearl of great value, he sold everything he owned and bought it!"

MATTHEW 13:45-46

REFLECTION

The merchant was earnestly searching for a pearl of great value, and when he found it, he sold everything he had to purchase it.

"The Kingdom of God can't be detected by visible signs. You won't be able to say, 'Here it is!' or 'It's over there!' For the Kingdom of God is already among you."

LUKE 17:20-21

REFLECTION

The Pharisees asked when
God's Kingdom would come,
not knowing that it had already
arrived. The Kingdom of God
is not like an earthly kingdom
with geographical boundaries.
Instead, it begins with the work
of God's Spirit in people's lives
and in relationships. We must
resist looking to institutions or
programs for evidence of the
progress of God's Kingdom.
Instead, we should look for what
God is doing in people's hearts.

Entering the Kingdom

"You can enter God's Kingdom only through the narrow gate. The highway to hell is broad, and its gate is wide for the many who choose that way. But the gateway to life is very narrow and the road is difficult, and only a few ever find it."

MATTHEW 7:13-14

REFLECTION

The narrowness of the gate does not mean that it is difficult to become a Christian but that there is only *one* way to eternal life with God and that only a few decide to walk that road. Believing in Jesus is the only way to heaven, because He alone died for our sins and made us right before God. Living His way may not be popular, but it is true and right. Thank God there is one way!

"Not everyone who calls out to me, 'Lord! Lord!' will enter the Kingdom of Heaven. Only those who actually do the will of my Father in heaven will enter. On judgment day many will say to me, 'Lord! Lord! We prophesied in your name and cast out demons in your name and per-formed many miracles in your name.' But I will reply, 'I never knew you. Get away from me, you who break God's laws.'"

MATTHEW 7:21-23

REFLECTION

Jesus exposed those people who sounded religious but had no personal relationship with Him. On "judgment day" only our relationship with Christ—our acceptance of Him as Savior and our obedience to Him—will matter. Many people think that if they are "good" people and say religious things, they will be rewarded with eternal life. In reality, faith in Christ is what will count at the judgment.

"Everyone who acknowledges me publicly here on earth, I will also acknowledge before my Father in heaven. But everyone who denies me here on earth, I will also deny before my Father in heaven."

MATTHEW 10:32-33

REFLECTION

We can reject Jesus now and be
rejected by Him at His second
coming, or we can accept Him
now and be accepted by Him
then. Rejecting Christ may help
us escape shame for the time
being, but it will guarantee an
eternity of shame later.

"Let the children come to me. Don't
stop them! For the Kingdom of God
belongs to those who are like these
children. I tell you the truth, anyone
who doesn't receive the Kingdom of
God like a child will never enter it."

MARK 10:14-15

REFLECTION

To feel secure, all children need
is a loving look and gentle
touch from someone who cares.

They believe us because they trust us. Jesus said that people should trust in Him with this kind of childlike faith. We do not have to understand all the mysteries of the universe; it is enough to know that God loves us and provides forgiveness for our sin.

"How hard it is for the rich to enter the Kingdom of God!" This amazed [the disciples]. But Jesus said again, "Dear children, it is very hard to enter the Kingdom of God. In fact, it is easier for a camel to go through the eye of a needle than for a rich person to enter the Kingdom of God! . . . Humanly speaking, it is impossible. But not with God. Everything is possible with God."

MARK 10:23-25, 27

REFLECTION

Jesus said it was very difficult for the rich to enter the Kingdom of God because the rich, having their basic physical needs met, often become self-reliant. When they feel empty, they buy something new to try to fill the void that only God can fill. Their abundance and self-sufficiency become their deficiency. The person who has everything on earth can still lack what is most important— eternal life.

"I assure you, no one can enter the Kingdom of God without being born of water and the Spirit. Humans can reproduce only human life, but the Holy Spirit gives birth to spiritual life. So don't be surprised when I say, 'You must be born again.' The wind blows wherever it wants. Just as you can hear the wind but can't tell where it comes from or where it is going, so you can't explain how people are born of the Spirit."

JOHN 3:5-8

REFLECTION

"Being born of water and the Spirit" could refer to (1) the contrast between physical birth (water) and spiritual birth (Spirit), or (2) being regenerated by the Spirit and signifying that rebirth by Christian baptism. The water may also represent the cleansing action of God's Holy Spirit. Jesus was explaining the importance of a spiritual rebirth, saying that people don't enter the Kingdom by living a better life, but by being spiritually reborn.

OTHER
TEACHINGS
OF JESUS

Don't Criticize Others

"Do not judge others, and you will not be judged. Do not condemn others, or it will all come back against you. Forgive others, and you will be forgiven. Give, and you will receive. Your gift will return to you in full—pressed down, shaken together to make room for more, running over, and poured into your lap. The amount you give will determine the amount you get back."

LUKE 6:37-38

REFLECTION

A forgiving spirit demonstrates
that a person has received
God's forgiveness. Jesus used
the picture of measuring grain
in a basket to ensure the full
amount. If we are critical rather
than compassionate, we will also
receive criticism. If we treat others generously, graciously, and
compassionately, however, these
qualities will come back to us
in full measure. We are to love
others, not judge them.

"Why worry about a speck in your
friend's eye when you have a log in
your own? How can you think of saying, 'Friend, let me help you get rid
of that speck in your eye,' when you
can't see past the log in your own eye?
Hypocrite! First get rid of the log in

**your own eye; then you will see well
enough to deal with the speck in your
friend's eye."**

LUKE 6:41-42

REFLECTION

Jesus doesn't mean we should
ignore wrongdoing, but we
should not be so worried about
others' sins that we overlook
our own. We often rational-
ize our sins by pointing out the
same mistakes in others. What
kinds of specks in others' eyes
are the easiest for you to criticize? Remember your own "logs"
when you feel like criticizing,
and you may find that you have
less to say.

Don't Worry

"I tell you not to worry about every-day life—whether you have enough food and drink, or enough clothes to wear. Isn't life more than food, and your body more than clothing? Look at the birds. They don't plant or harvest or store food in barns, for your heavenly Father feeds them. And aren't you far more valuable to him than they are? Can all your worries add a single moment to your life?

"And why worry about your clothing? Look at the lilies of the field and how they grow. They don't work or make their clothing, yet Solomon in all his glory was not dressed as beautifully as they are. And if God cares so wonderfully for wildflowers that are here today and thrown into the fire tomorrow, he will certainly care for you. Why do you have so little faith?"

MATTHEW 6:25-30

REFLECTION

Jesus tells us not to worry about those needs that God promises to supply. Worry may (1) damage your health, (2) disrupt your productivity, (3) negatively affect the way you treat others, and (4) reduce your ability to trust in God. How many ill effects of worry are you experiencing? Here is the difference between worry and genuine concern—worry immobilizes, but concern moves you to action.

"**Don't worry about tomorrow, for tomorrow will bring its own worries. Today's trouble is enough for today.**"

MATTHEW 6:34

REFLECTION

Planning for tomorrow is time well spent; worrying about tomorrow is time wasted. Sometimes it's difficult to tell the difference. Worriers are consumed by fear and find it difficult to trust God. They let their plans interfere with their relationship with God. By contrast, careful planning is thinking ahead about goals, steps, and schedules, and trusting in God's guidance.

"These things dominate the thoughts of unbelievers all over the world, but your Father already knows your needs. Seek the Kingdom of God above all else, and he will give you everything you need."

LUKE 12:30-31

REFLECTION

Seeking the Kingdom of God above all else means making Jesus the Lord and King of your life. He must control every area— your work, play, plans, relationships. Is the Kingdom only one of your many concerns, or is it central to all you do? Are you holding back any areas of your life from God's control? As Lord and Creator, He wants to help provide what you need as well as guide how you use what He provides.

"Don't be afraid of those who want to kill your body; they cannot touch your soul. Fear only God, who can destroy both soul and body in hell. What is the price of two sparrows— one copper coin? But not a single sparrow can fall to the ground without your Father knowing it. And the very hairs on your head are all numbered. So don't be afraid; you are more valuable to God than a whole flock of sparrows."

MATTHEW 10:28-31

REFLECTION

Jesus said that God is aware of everything that happens even to sparrows, and you are far more valuable to Him than they are. You are so valuable that God sent His only Son to die for you. Because God places such value on you, you need never fear personal threats or difficult trials. These can't shake God's love or dislodge His Spirit from within you.

This doesn't mean, however, that God will take away all your troubles. The real test of value is how well something holds up under the wear, tear, and stress of everyday life. Those who stand up for Christ in spite of their troubles truly have lasting value and will receive great rewards.

Eternal Life

"This is the way to have eternal life—to know you, the only true God, and Jesus Christ, the one you sent to earth."

JOHN 17:3

REFLECTION

How do we get eternal life? Jesus tells us clearly here—by knowing God the Father Himself through His Son, Jesus Christ. Eternal life requires entering into a personal relationship with God in Jesus Christ. When we admit our sin and turn away from it, Christ's love lives in us by the Holy Spirit.

"I tell you the truth, those who listen to my message and believe in God who sent me have eternal life. They will never be condemned for their sins, but they have already passed from death into life."

JOHN 5:24

REFLECTION

Eternal life—living forever with God—begins when you accept Jesus Christ as Savior. At that moment, new life begins in you. It is a completed transaction. You still will face physical death, but when Christ returns again, your body will be resurrected to live forever.

"It is my Father's will that all who see his Son and believe in him should have eternal life. I will raise them up at the last day."

JOHN 6:40

REFLECTION

Those who put their faith in Christ will be resurrected from physical death to eternal life with God when Christ comes again.

"I tell you the truth, anyone who believes has eternal life. Yes, I am the bread of life! Your ancestors ate manna in the wilderness, but they all died. Anyone who eats the bread from heaven, however, will never die. I am the living bread that came down from heaven. Anyone who eats this bread will live forever; and this bread, which I will offer so the world may live, is my flesh."

JOHN 6:47-51

REFLECTION

Here Jesus refers to the manna
that God had given their ancestors in the wilderness during
Moses' time. This bread was
physical and temporal. The people ate it, and it sustained them
for a day. But they had to get
more bread every day, and this
bread could not keep them from
dying. Jesus, who is much greater
than Moses, offers Himself as the
spiritual bread from heaven that
satisfies completely and leads to
eternal life.

Hearing and Obeying

"Anyone who listens to my teaching and follows it is wise, like a person who builds a house on solid rock. Though the rain comes in torrents and the floodwaters rise and the winds beat against that house, it won't collapse because it is built on bedrock. But anyone who hears my teaching and doesn't obey it is foolish, like a person who builds a house on sand. When the rains and floods come and the winds beat against that house, it will collapse with a mighty crash."

MATTHEW 7:24-27

REFLECTION

To build "on solid rock" means to be a hearing, responding disciple, not a phony, superficial one. Practicing obedience becomes the solid foundation to weather the storms of life.

"What do you think about this? A man with two sons told the older boy, 'Son, go out and work in the vineyard today.' The son answered, 'No, I won't go,' but later he changed his mind and went anyway. Then the father told the other son, 'You go,' and he said, 'Yes, sir, I will.' But he didn't go.

"Which of the two obeyed his father?"

MATTHEW 21:28-31

REFLECTION

The son who said he would obey
and then didn't represented many
of the people of Israel in Jesus'
day, particularly the religious leaders. They said they wanted to do
God's will, but they constantly
disobeyed. They were phony, just
going through the motions. It
is dangerous to pretend to obey
God when our hearts are far from
Him because God knows our
true intentions. Our actions must
match our words.

"A farmer went out to plant his seed.
As he scattered it across his field,
some seed fell on a footpath, where it
was stepped on, and the birds ate it.
Other seed fell among rocks. It began
to grow, but the plant soon wilted
and died for lack of moisture. Other

seed fell among thorns that grew up
with it and choked out the tender
plants. Still other seed fell on fertile
soil. This seed grew and produced
a crop that was a hundred times as
much as had been planted!" When
[Jesus] had said this, he called out,
"Anyone with ears to hear should listen and understand. . . .

"This is the meaning of the
parable: The seed is God's word.
The seeds that fell on the footpath
represent those who hear the
message, only to have the devil come
and take it away from their hearts
and prevent them from believing
and being saved. The seeds on the
rocky soil represent those who hear
the message and receive it with joy.
But since they don't have deep roots,
they believe for a while, then they
fall away when they face temptation.

The seeds that fell among the
thorns represent those who hear
the message, but all too quickly the
message is crowded out by the cares
and riches and pleasures of this
life. And so they never grow into
maturity. And the seeds that fell on
the good soil represent honest, good-
hearted people who hear God's word,
cling to it, and patiently produce a
huge harvest."

LUKE 8:5-8, 11-15

REFLECTION

"Footpath" people, like many
of the Jewish religious leaders of
Jesus' day, refuse to believe God's
message. "Rocky soil" people,
like many in the crowds who followed Jesus, believe His message
but never get around to doing
anything about it. "Thorn patch"
people, overcome by worries and

the lure of materialism, leave
no room in their lives for God.
"Good soil" people, in contrast
to all the other groups, follow
Jesus no matter what the cost.
Which type of soil are you?

Jesus and the Law

"Don't misunderstand why I have come. I did not come to abolish the law of Moses or the writings of the prophets. No, I came to accomplish their purpose. I tell you the truth, until heaven and earth disappear, not even the smallest detail of God's law will disappear until its purpose is achieved. So if you ignore the least commandment and teach others to do the same, you will be called the least in the Kingdom of Heaven. But anyone who obeys God's laws and teaches them will be called great in the Kingdom of Heaven."

MATTHEW 5:17-19

REFLECTION

Some of those in the crowd were experts at telling others what to do, but they missed the central point of God's laws themselves. Jesus made it clear, however, that obeying God's laws is more important than explaining them. It's much easier to study God's laws and tell others to obey them than to put them into practice. How are you doing at obeying God *yourself*?

"You have heard that our ancestors were told, 'You must not murder. If you commit murder, you are subject to judgment.' But I say, if you are even angry with someone, you are subject to judgment! If you call someone an idiot, you are in danger of being brought before

the court. And if you curse someone, you are in danger of the fires
of hell."

MATTHEW 5:21-22

REFLECTION

When Jesus said, "But I say,"
He was not doing away with
the law or adding His own
beliefs. Rather, He was giving
a fuller understanding of why
God made that law in the first
place. For example, Moses said,
"You must not murder" (Exodus
20:13); Jesus taught that we
should not even become angry
enough to murder, for then we
have already committed murder
in our hearts. The Pharisees read
this law and, not having literally
murdered anyone, felt that they
had obeyed it. Yet they were
angry enough with Jesus that

they would soon plot His death, though they would not do the dirty work themselves. We miss the intent of God's Word when we read His rules for living without trying to understand why He made them. When do you keep God's rules but close your eyes to His intent?

"You have also heard that our ancestors were told, 'You must not break your vows; you must carry out the vows you make to the LORD.' But I say, do not make any vows! Do not say, 'By heaven!' because heaven is God's throne. And do not say, 'By the earth!' because the earth is his footstool. And do not say, 'By Jerusalem!' for Jerusalem is the city of the great King. Do not even say, 'By my head!' for you can't turn one hair white or black. Just say a simple, 'Yes, I will,' or 'No, I won't.' Anything beyond this is from the evil one."

MATTHEW 5:33-37

REFLECTION

Vows were common, but Jesus told His followers not to use them—their word alone should be enough. Are you known as a person of your word? Truthfulness seems so rare that we feel we must end our statements with "I promise." If we tell the truth all the time, we will have less pressure to back up our words with an oath or a promise.

"You have heard the law that says the punishment must match the injury: 'An eye for an eye, and a tooth for a tooth.' But I say, do not resist an evil person! If someone slaps you on the right cheek, offer the other cheek also. If you are sued in court and your shirt is taken from you, give your coat, too. If a soldier demands that you carry his gear for a mile, carry it two miles. Give to those who ask, and don't turn away from those who want to borrow."

MATTHEW 5:38-42

REFLECTION

To many Jews of Jesus' day, these statements were offensive. Any Messiah who would turn the other cheek was not the military leader they wanted to lead a revolt against Rome. Since they were under Roman oppression, they wanted retaliation against their enemies, whom they hated. But Jesus suggested a new, radical response to injustice: instead of demanding rights, give them up freely! According to Jesus, it is more important to *give* justice and mercy than to receive it.

"If you had a sheep that fell into a well on the Sabbath, wouldn't you work to pull it out? Of course you would. And how much more valuable is a person than a sheep! Yes, the law permits a person to do good on the Sabbath."

MATTHEW 12:11-12

REFLECTION

The Pharisees placed their laws above human need. They were so concerned about Jesus breaking one of their rules that they did not care about the man's deformed hand. What is your attitude toward others? If your convictions don't allow you to help certain people, your convictions may not be in tune with God's Word. Don't allow rule keeping to blind you to human need.

"Haven't you ever read in the Scriptures what David did when he and his companions were hungry? He went into the house of God (during the days when Abiathar was high priest) and broke the law by eating the sacred loaves of bread that only the priests are allowed to eat. He also gave some to his companions. . . . The Sabbath was made to meet the needs of people, and not people to meet the requirements of the Sabbath. So the Son of Man is Lord, even over the Sabbath!"

MARK 2:25-28

REFLECTION

God created the Sabbath for our benefit; we are restored both physically and spiritually when we take time to rest and to focus on God. For the Pharisees, Sabbath rules had become more important than Sabbath rest. Both David and Jesus understood that the intent of God's law is to promote love for God and others.

Jesus and the Law

and others.

Marriage and Divorce

"You have heard the commandment that says, 'You must not commit adultery.' But I say, anyone who even looks at a woman with lust has already committed adultery with her in his heart. So if your eye—even your good eye—causes you to lust, gouge it out and throw it away. It is better for you to lose one part of your body than for your whole body to be thrown into hell. And if your hand—even your stronger hand—causes you to sin, cut it off and throw it away. It is better for you to lose one part of

your body than for your whole body to be thrown into hell."

MATTHEW 5:27-30

REFLECTION

The Old Testament law said that it is wrong for a person to have sex with someone other than his or her spouse. But Jesus said that feeding the *desire* to have sex with someone other than your spouse is mental adultery and thus sin. Jesus emphasized that if the *act* is wrong, then so is the *intention*. To be faithful to your spouse with your body but not your mind is to break the trust so vital to a strong marriage. Jesus is not condemning natural interest in the opposite sex or even healthy sexual desire but the deliberate and repeated filling of one's mind with fantasies that would be evil if acted out.

"You have heard the law that says,
'A man can divorce his wife by merely
giving her a written notice of divorce.'
But I say that a man who divorces
his wife, unless she has been unfaithful, causes her to commit adultery.
And anyone who marries a divorced
woman also commits adultery."

MATTHEW 5:31-32

REFLECTION

Divorce is as hurtful and destruc-
tive today as it was in Jesus' day.
God intends marriage to be a lifetime commitment. When entering into marriage, people should
never consider divorce an option
for solving problems or a way
out of a relationship that seems
dead. In these verses, Jesus is also
attacking those who purposefully
abuse the marriage contract, using
divorce to satisfy their lustful

desire to marry someone else. Are your actions today helping your marriage grow stronger, or are you tearing it apart?

"Whoever divorces his wife and marries someone else commits adultery against her. And if a woman divorces her husband and marries someone else, she commits adultery."

MARK 10:11-12

REFLECTION

Don't enter marriage with the option of getting out. Your marriage is more likely to be happy if from the outset you are committed to permanence. Don't be hard-hearted like these Pharisees, but be hardheaded in your determination, with God's help, to stay together.

"Haven't you read the Scriptures? . . . They record that from the beginning 'God made them male and female. . . . This explains why a man leaves his father and mother and is joined to his wife, and the two are united into one.' Since they are no longer two but one, let no one split apart what God has joined together. . . .

"Moses permitted divorce only as a concession to your hard hearts, but it was not what God had originally intended. And I tell you this, whoever divorces his wife and marries someone else commits adultery— unless his wife has been unfaithful."

MATTHEW 19:4-9

REFLECTION

Jesus' cousin John had been put in prison and killed at least in part for his public opinions on marriage and divorce, so the Pharisees hoped to trap Jesus, too. They were trying to trick Jesus by having Him choose sides in a theological controversy. Two schools of thought represented two opposing views of divorce. One group supported divorce for almost any reason. The other believed that divorce could be allowed only for marital unfaithfulness. This conflict hinged on how each group interpreted Deuteronomy 24:1-4. In His answer, however, Jesus focused on marriage rather than divorce. He pointed out that God intended marriage to be permanent and gave four reasons for the importance of marriage.

Money and Possessions

"Don't store up treasures here on earth, where moths eat them and rust destroys them, and where thieves break in and steal. Store your treasures in heaven, where moths and rust cannot destroy, and thieves do not break in and steal. Wherever your treasure is, there the desires of your heart will also be."

MATTHEW 6:19-21

REFLECTION

Jesus contrasted heavenly values with earthly values when He explained that our first loyalty should be to those things that do not fade, cannot be stolen or used up, and never wear out. Storing treasures in heaven is not limited to tithing but is accomplished by all acts of obedience to God. There is a sense in which giving our money to God's work is like investing in heaven. But we should seek to please God not only in our giving but also in fulfilling God's purposes in all we do.

"No one can serve two masters. For you will hate one and love the other; you will be devoted to one and despise the other. You cannot serve both God and money."

MATTHEW 6:24

REFLECTION

We should not be fascinated with our possessions, lest *they* possess *us*. This may mean we have to do some cutting back if our possessions are becoming too important to us. Jesus calls for a decision that allows us to live contentedly with whatever we have because we have chosen eternal values over temporary, earthly treasures.

"Don't worry about these things, saying, 'What will we eat? What will we drink? What will we wear?' These things dominate the thoughts of unbelievers, but your heavenly Father already knows all your needs. Seek the Kingdom of God above all else, and live righteously, and he will give you everything you need."

MATTHEW 6:31-33

REFLECTION

To "seek the Kingdom of God above all else" means to put God first in your life, to fill your thoughts with His desires, to take His character for your pattern, and to serve and obey Him in everything. What is really important to you? People, objects, goals, and other desires all compete for priority. Any of these can quickly become most important to you if you don't actively choose to give God first place in *every* area of your life.

"I tell you the truth, it is very hard for a rich person to enter the Kingdom of Heaven. I'll say it again—it is easier for a camel to go through the eye of a needle than for a rich person to enter the Kingdom of God!"

MATTHEW 19:23-24

REFLECTION

Because it is impossible for a camel to go through the eye of a needle, it appears impossible for a rich person to get into the Kingdom of God. The disciples were astounded. They thought that if anyone could be saved, it would be the rich, whom their culture considered especially blessed by God. Jesus explained, however, that "with God everything is possible" (Matthew 19:26). Even rich people can enter the Kingdom if God brings them in. Faith in Christ, not in self or riches, is what counts. On what are you counting for salvation?

"What sorrow awaits you who are rich, for you have your only happiness now.

What sorrow awaits you who are
      fat and prosperous now,
   for a time of awful hunger
      awaits you.
What sorrow awaits you who
      laugh now,
   for your laughing will turn to
      mourning and sorrow."

LUKE 6:24-25

REFLECTION

If you are trying to find fulfillment only through riches, wealth
may be the only reward you will
ever get—and it does not last.
We should not seek comfort now
at the expense of eternal life.

"A rich man had a fertile farm that
produced fine crops. He said to himself, 'What should I do? I don't have
room for all my crops.' Then he said,
'I know! I'll tear down my barns and

build bigger ones. Then I'll have room enough to store all my wheat and other goods. And I'll sit back and say to myself, "My friend, you have enough stored away for years to come. Now take it easy! Eat, drink, and be merry!"'

"But God said to him, 'You fool! You will die this very night. Then who will get everything you worked for?'

"Yes, a person is a fool to store up earthly wealth but not have a rich relationship with God."

LUKE 12:16-21

REFLECTION

The rich man in Jesus' story died before he could begin to use what was stored in his big barns. Planning for retirement—preparing for life *before* death—is wise, but neglecting life *after* death is disastrous. If you accumulate wealth only to enrich yourself, with no concern for helping others, you will enter eternity empty handed.

"There was a certain rich man who was splendidly clothed in purple and fine linen and who lived each day in luxury. At his gate lay a poor man named Lazarus who was covered with sores. As Lazarus lay there longing for scraps from the rich man's table, the dogs would come and lick his open sores.

"Finally, the poor man died and was carried by the angels to be with Abraham. The rich man also died and was buried, and his soul went to the place of the dead. There, in torment, he saw Abraham in the far distance with Lazarus at his side.

"The rich man shouted, 'Father

Abraham, have some pity! Send Lazarus over here to dip the tip of his finger in water and cool my tongue. I am in anguish in these flames.'

"But Abraham said to him, 'Son, remember that during your lifetime you had everything you wanted, and Lazarus had nothing. So now he is here being comforted, and you are in anguish. And besides, there is a great chasm separating us. No one can cross over to you from here, and no one can cross over to us from there.'

"Then the rich man said, 'Please, Father Abraham, at least send him to my father's home. For I have five brothers, and I want him to warn them so they don't end up in this place of torment.'

"But Abraham said, 'Moses and the prophets have warned them. Your brothers can read what they wrote.'

"The rich man replied, 'No, Father Abraham! But if someone is sent to them from the dead, then they will repent of their sins and turn to God.'

"But Abraham said, 'If they won't listen to Moses and the prophets, they won't be persuaded even if someone rises from the dead.'"

LUKE 16:19-31

REFLECTION

The Pharisees considered wealth to be a proof of a person's righteousness. Jesus startled them with this story, in which a diseased beggar is rewarded and a rich man is punished. The rich man did not go to hell because of his wealth but because he was selfish, refusing to feed Lazarus, take him in, or care for him. The rich man was hard hearted in spite of his great blessings. The amount of money we have is not as important as the way we use it. What is your attitude toward your money and possessions? Do you hoard them selfishly, or do you use them to help others?

Overcoming Temptation

"What sorrow awaits the world, because it tempts people to sin. Temptations are inevitable, but what sorrow awaits the person who does the tempting. So if your hand or foot causes you to sin, cut it off and throw it away. It's better to enter eternal life with only one hand or one foot than to be thrown into eternal fire with both of your hands and feet. And if your eye causes you to sin, gouge it out and throw it away. It's better to enter eternal life with only one eye than to have two eyes and be thrown into the fire of hell."

MATTHEW 18:7-9

REFLECTION

We must remove stumbling
blocks that cause us to sin.
However, this does not mean
to cut off a part of the body.
For the church it means that
any person, program, or teaching that threatens the spiritual
growth of the body must be
removed. For the individual, any
relationship, practice, or activ-
ity that leads to sin should be
stopped. Jesus says it would be
better to go to heaven with one
hand than to hell with both. Sin,
of course, affects more than our
hands; it affects our minds and
hearts.

**One day Jesus said to his disciples,
"There will always be temptations to
sin, but what sorrow awaits the person**

who does the tempting! It would be better to be thrown into the sea with a millstone hung around your neck than to cause one of these little ones to fall into sin. So watch yourselves!

"If another believer sins, rebuke that person; then if there is repentance, forgive."

LUKE 17:1-3

REFLECTION

Jesus may have been directing this warning at the religious leaders who taught their converts their own hypocritical ways. They were perpetuating an evil system. A person who teaches others has a solemn responsibility. Like a physician, a teacher should keep this ancient oath in mind: "First, do no harm."

"Keep watch and pray, so that you will not give in to temptation. For the spirit is willing, but the body is weak!"

MATTHEW 26:41

REFLECTION

The way to overcome temptation is to keep alert and pray. Keeping alert means being aware of the possibilities of temptation, sensitive to its subtleties, and spiritually equipped to fight it. Because temptation strikes where we are most vulnerable, we can't resist it alone. Prayer is essential because God's strength can shore up our defenses and defeat Satan's power.

"Pray that you will not give in to temptation."

LUKE 22:40

REFLECTION

Jesus asked the disciples to pray that they would not fall into temptation because He knew that He would soon be leaving them. Jesus also knew that they would need extra strength to face the temptations ahead—temptations to run away or to deny their relationship with Him. They were about to see Jesus die. Would they still think He was the Messiah? The disciples' strongest temptation would undoubtedly be to think they had been deceived.

Restoring Relationships

"If you are presenting a sacrifice at the altar in the Temple and you suddenly remember that someone has something against you, leave your sacrifice there at the altar. Go and be reconciled to that person. Then come and offer your sacrifice to God.

"When you are on the way to court with your adversary, settle your differences quickly. Otherwise, your accuser may hand you over to the judge, who will hand you over to an officer, and you will be thrown into prison. And if that happens, you surely won't be free again until you have paid the last penny."

MATTHEW 5:23-26

REFLECTION

Broken relationships can hinder our relationship with God. If we have a problem or grievance with a friend, we should resolve the problem as soon as possible. We are hypocrites if we claim to love God while we hate others. Our attitudes toward others reflect our relationship with God.

"Do not judge others, and you will not be judged. For you will be treated as you treat others. The standard you use in judging is the standard by which you will be judged.

"And why worry about a speck

in your friend's eye when you have
a log in your own? How can you
think of saying to your friend, 'Let
me help you get rid of that speck in
your eye,' when you can't see past
the log in your own eye? Hypocrite!
First get rid of the log in your own
eye; then you will see well enough
to deal with the speck in your
friend's eye."

MATTHEW 7:1-5

REFLECTION

Jesus' statement "Do not judge
others" refers to the kind of
hypocritical, judgmental attitude
that tears others down in order
to build oneself up. It is not a
blanket statement to overlook
wrong behavior of others but a
call to be *discerning* rather than
negative. Jesus said to expose
false prophets, and Paul taught

that we should exercise church discipline and trust God to be the final Judge.

"If another believer sins against you, go privately and point out the offense. If the other person listens and confesses it, you have won that person back. But if you are unsuccessful, take one or two others with you and go back again, so that everything you say may be confirmed by two or three witnesses. If the person still refuses to listen, take your case to the church. Then if he or she won't accept the church's decision, treat that person as a pagan or a corrupt tax collector."

MATTHEW 18:15-17

REFLECTION

When someone wrongs us, we often do the opposite of what Jesus recommends. We turn away in hatred or resentment, seek revenge, or engage in gossip. By contrast, we should go to that person *first*, as difficult as that may be. Then we should forgive that person as often as he or she needs it. This will create a much better chance of restoring the relationship.

"Watch yourselves!

"If another believer sins, rebuke that person; then if there is repentance, forgive. Even if that person wrongs you seven times a day and each time turns again and asks forgiveness, you must forgive."

Luke 17:3-4

REFLECTION

To rebuke does not mean to point out every sin we see; it means to bring sin to a person's attention with the purpose of restoring him or her to God and to fellow humans. When you feel you must rebuke another Christian for a sin, check your attitudes before you speak. Do you love that person? Are you willing to forgive? Unless rebuke is tied to forgiveness, it will not help the sinning person.

Satan and Evil Spirits

"Any kingdom divided by civil war is doomed. A town or family splintered by feuding will fall apart. And if Satan is casting out Satan, he is divided and fighting against himself. His own kingdom will not survive. And if I am empowered by Satan, what about your own exorcists? They cast out demons, too, so they will condemn you for what you have said. But if I am casting out demons by the Spirit of God, then the Kingdom of God has arrived among you. For who is powerful enough to enter the house of a strong man like Satan and plunder his goods? Only someone even stronger—someone who could tie him up and then plunder his house."

MATTHEW 12:25-29

REFLECTION

At Jesus' birth, Satan's power and control were disrupted. In the wilderness Jesus overcame Satan's temptations, and at the Resurrection He defeated Satan's ultimate weapon—death. Eventually Satan will be constrained forever, and evil will no longer pervade the earth. Jesus has complete power and authority over Satan and all his forces.

"When an evil spirit leaves a person, it goes into the desert, seeking rest but finding none. Then it says, 'I will return to the person I came from.' So it returns and finds its former home empty, swept, and in order. Then the spirit finds seven other spirits more evil than itself, and they all enter the person and live there. And so that person is worse off than before. That will be the experience of this evil generation."

MATTHEW 12:43-45

REFLECTION

Jesus was describing the attitude of the nation of Israel and the religious leaders in particular. Just cleaning up one's life without filling it with God leaves plenty of room for Satan to enter. The book of Ezra records how the people rid themselves of idolatry but failed to replace it with love for God and obedience to Him. Ridding our lives of sin is the first step. We must also take the second step: filling our lives with God's Word and the Holy Spirit. Unfilled and complacent people are easy targets for Satan.

"I saw Satan fall from heaven like lightning! Look, I have given you authority over all the power of the enemy, and you can walk among snakes and scorpions and crush them. Nothing will injure you. But don't rejoice because evil spirits obey you; rejoice because your names are registered in heaven."

LUKE 10:18-20

REFLECTION

Jesus may have been looking ahead to His victory over Satan at the cross. John 12:31-32 indicates that Satan would be judged and driven out at the time of Jesus' death. On the other hand, Jesus may have been warning His disciples against pride. Perhaps He was referring to Isaiah 14:12-17, which begins, "How you are fallen from heaven, O shining star, son of the morning!" Some interpreters identify these verses with Satan and explain that Satan's pride led to all the evil we see on earth today. To Jesus' disciples, who were thrilled with their power over evil spirits, He may have been giving this stern warning: "Yours is the kind of pride that led to Satan's downfall. Be careful!"

The Power of Faith

"I tell you the truth, I haven't seen faith like this in all Israel! And I tell you this, that many Gentiles will come from all over the world—from east and west—and sit down with Abraham, Isaac, and Jacob at the feast in the Kingdom of Heaven. But many Israelites—those for whom the Kingdom was prepared—will be thrown into outer darkness, where there will be weeping and gnashing of teeth."

MATTHEW 8:10-12

REFLECTION

Jesus told the crowd that many
religious Jews who should be in
the Kingdom would be excluded
because of their lack of faith.
Entrenched in their religious
traditions, they could not accept
Christ and His new message. We
must be careful not to become so
set in our religious habits that we
expect God to work only in speci-
fied ways. Don't limit God by
your mind-set and lack of faith.

**"Daughter, be encouraged! Your faith
has made you well."**

MATTHEW 9:22

REFLECTION

The woman Jesus was speaking
to had suffered for twelve years
with a hemorrhage. In our times
of desperation, we don't have

to worry about the correct way to reach out to God. Like this woman, we can simply reach out in faith. He will respond.

"You don't have enough faith. . . . I tell you the truth, if you had faith even as small as a mustard seed, you could say to this mountain, 'Move from here to there,' and it would move. Nothing would be impossible."

MATTHEW 17:20

REFLECTION

Jesus wasn't condemning the disciples for substandard faith; He was trying to show how important faith would be in their future ministry. If you are facing a problem that seems as big and immovable as a mountain, turn your eyes from the mountain and look to Christ for more faith.

Only then will you be able to overcome the obstacles that may stand in your way.

"Anything is possible if a person believes."

MARK 9:23

REFLECTION

Jesus' words do not mean that we can automatically obtain anything we want if we just think positively. Jesus meant that anything is *possible* if we believe, because nothing is too difficult for God. We cannot have everything we pray for as if by magic, but with faith, we can have everything we need to serve Him.

"Your faith has saved you; go in peace."

LUKE 7:50

REFLECTION

The Pharisees believed that only
God could forgive sins, so they
wondered why this man, Jesus,
was saying that the woman's
sins were forgiven. They did
not grasp the fact that Jesus is
indeed God.

"If you had faith even as small as a
mustard seed, you could say to this
mulberry tree, 'May you be uprooted
and thrown into the sea,' and it
would obey you!"

LUKE 17:6

REFLECTION

A mustard seed is small, but it is
alive and growing. Almost invisible at first, the seed will begin to
develop, first under the ground
and then visibly. Like a tiny seed,

a small amount of genuine faith in God will take root and grow. Although each change will be gradual and imperceptible, soon this faith will have produced major results that will uproot and destroy competing loyalties. We don't need more faith; a tiny seed of faith is enough if it is alive and growing.

The Way of Humility

"When you are invited to a wedding feast, don't sit in the seat of honor. What if someone who is more distinguished than you has also been invited? The host will come and say, 'Give this person your seat.' Then you will be embarrassed, and you will have to take whatever seat is left at the foot of the table!

"Instead, take the lowest place at the foot of the table. Then when your host sees you, he will come and say, 'Friend, we have a better place for you!' Then you will be honored in front of all the other guests. For

those who exalt themselves will be
humbled, and those who humble
themselves will be exalted."

LUKE 14:8-11

REFLECTION

How can we humble ourselves?
Some people try to give the
appearance of humility in order
to manipulate others. Others
think that humility means putting themselves down. Truly
humble people compare themselves only with Christ, realize
their sinfulness, and understand
their limitations. On the other
hand, they also recognize their
gifts and strengths and are willing to use them as Christ directs.
Humility is not self-degradation;
it is realistic self-assessment and
commitment to serve.

"If you try to hang on to your life, you will lose it. But if you give up your life for my sake, you will save it. And what do you benefit if you gain the whole world but lose your own soul? Is anything worth more than your soul?"

MATTHEW 16:25-26

REFLECTION

The possibility of losing their lives was very real for the disciples as well as for Jesus. Real discipleship implies real commitment—pledging our whole existence to His service. If we try to save our physical life from death, pain, or discomfort, we may risk losing eternal life. If we protect ourselves from the pain God calls us to suffer, we begin to die spiritually and emotionally. Our lives turn inward, and we lose our intended purpose. When we give our lives in service to Christ, however, we discover the real purpose of living.

True Happiness

"God blesses those who are poor
    and realize their need for him,
  for the Kingdom of Heaven is
    theirs.
God blesses those who mourn,
  for they will be comforted.
God blesses those who are humble,
  for they will inherit the whole
    earth.
God blesses those who hunger and
    thirst for justice,
  for they will be satisfied.
God blesses those who are merciful,
  for they will be shown mercy.

God blesses those whose hearts
  are pure,
    for they will see God.
God blesses those who work for
  peace,
    for they will be called the
    children of God.
God blesses those who are
  persecuted for doing right,
    for the Kingdom of Heaven is
    theirs.

"God blesses you when people
mock you and persecute you and lie
about you and say all sorts of evil
things against you because you are
my followers. Be happy about it! Be
very glad! For a great reward awaits
you in heaven. And remember, the
ancient prophets were persecuted in
the same way."

MATTHEW 5:3-12

REFLECTION

Each beatitude tells how to be
blessed by God. Being blessed
means more than happiness. It
implies the fortunate or enviable
state of those who are in God's
Kingdom. The Beatitudes don't
promise laughter, pleasure, or
earthly prosperity. Being blessed
by God means the experience
of hope and joy, independent of
outward circumstances. To find
hope and joy, the deepest form of
happiness, follow Jesus no matter
what the cost.

"**God blesses you who are poor,**
 for the Kingdom of God is yours.
God blesses you who are hungry
   now,
 for you will be satisfied.
God blesses you who weep now,
 for in due time you will laugh.

What blessings await you when people hate you and exclude you and mock you and curse you as evil because you follow the Son of Man. When that happens, be happy! Yes, leap for joy! For a great reward awaits you in heaven. And remember, their ancestors treated the ancient prophets that same way."

LUKE 6:20-23

REFLECTION

These verses are called the *Beatitudes*, from the Latin word meaning "blessing." They describe what it means to be Christ's follower, give standards of conduct, and contrast Kingdom values with worldly values, showing what Christ's followers can expect from the world and what God will give them. In addition, they contrast fake piety with true humility. They also show how Old Testament expectations are fulfilled in God's Kingdom.

"You believe because you have seen me. Blessed are those who believe without seeing me."

JOHN 20:29

REFLECTION

Some people think they would believe in Jesus if they could see a definite sign or miracle. But Jesus says we are blessed if we can believe without seeing. We have all the proof we need in the words of the Bible and the testimony of believers. A physical appearance would not make Jesus any more real to us than He is now.

True Riches

"If you give even a cup of cold water to one of the least of my followers, you will surely be rewarded."

MATTHEW 10:42

REFLECTION

How much we love God can be measured by how well we treat others. Jesus' example of giving a cup of cold water to someone who thirsts is a good model of unselfish service. A child usually can't or won't return a favor. God notices every good deed we do or don't do as if He were the one receiving it. Is there something unselfish you can do for someone else today? Although no one else may see you, God will notice.

"If you want to be perfect, go and sell all your possessions and give the money to the poor, and you will have treasure in heaven. Then come, follow me."

MATTHEW 19:21

REFLECTION

Should all believers sell everything they own? No. We are responsible to care for our own needs and the needs of our families so as not to be a burden on others. We should, however, be willing to give up anything if God asks us to do so. This kind of attitude allows nothing to come between us and God and keeps us from using our

God-given wealth selfishly. If you are relieved by the fact that Christ did not tell all His followers to sell all their possessions, then you may be too attached to what you have.

"Why criticize this woman for doing such a good thing to me? You will always have the poor among you, but you will not always have me. She has poured this perfume on me to prepare my body for burial. I tell you the truth, wherever the Good News is preached throughout the world, this woman's deed will be remembered and discussed."

MATTHEW 26:10-13

REFLECTION

Here Jesus brought back to mind Deuteronomy 15:11: "There will always be some in the land who are poor." This statement does not justify ignoring the needs of the poor. Scripture continually exhorts us to care for the needy. The passage in Deuteronomy continues: "That is why I am commanding you to share freely with the poor and with other Israelites in need." Rather, by saying this, Jesus highlighted the special sacrifice Mary made for Him.

"Seek the Kingdom of God above all else, and he will give you everything you need.

"So don't be afraid, little flock. For it gives your Father great happiness to give you the Kingdom.

"Sell your possessions and give to those in need. This will store up treasure for you in heaven! And the purses of heaven never get old or develop holes. Your treasure will be safe; no thief can steal it and no moth can destroy it. Wherever your treasure is, there the desires of your heart will also be."

Luke 12:31-34

Reflection

Money seen as an end in itself quickly traps us and cuts us off from both God and the needy. The key to using money wisely is to see how much we can use for God's purposes, not how much we can accumulate for ourselves. Does God's love touch your wallet? Does your money free you to help others? If so, you are storing up lasting treasures in heaven. If your financial goals and possessions hinder you from giving generously, loving others, or serving God, sell what you must to bring your life into line with His purposes.

"I tell you the truth," Jesus said, "this poor widow has given more than all the rest of them. For they have given a tiny part of their surplus, but she, poor as she is, has given everything she has."

LUKE 21:3-4

REFLECTION

In contrast to the way most of us handle our money, this widow gave all she had to live on. When we consider ourselves generous in giving a small percentage of our income to the Lord, we resemble those who gave "a tiny part of their surplus." Here, Jesus admired the woman's generous and sacrificial giving. As believers, we should consider increasing our giving—whether money, time, or talents—to a point beyond convenience or comfort.

True Righteousness

"I warn you—unless your righteousness is better than the righteousness of the teachers of religious law and the Pharisees, you will never enter the Kingdom of Heaven!"

MATTHEW 5:20

REFLECTION

The Pharisees were exacting and scrupulous in their attempts to follow their laws. So how could Jesus reasonably call us to greater righteousness than theirs? The Pharisees' weakness was that they were content to obey the laws outwardly without allowing God to change their hearts (or attitudes). Jesus was saying that His listeners needed a different kind of righteousness altogether, motivated by a love for God, not just a more intense version of the Pharisees' legal compliance. The Pharisees looked pious, but they were far from the Kingdom of Heaven. God judges our hearts as well as our deeds, for it is in the heart that our real allegiance lies. Spend more time thinking about your attitudes that people don't see than your actions that are seen by all.

"Watch out! Don't do your good deeds publicly, to be admired by others, for you will lose the reward from your Father in heaven. When you give to someone in need, don't do as the

hypocrites do—blowing trumpets
in the synagogues and streets to call
attention to their acts of charity! I
tell you the truth, they have received
all the reward they will ever get. But
when you give to someone in need,
don't let your left hand know what
your right hand is doing. Give your
gifts in private, and your Father, who
sees everything, will reward you."

MATTHEW 6:1-4

REFLECTION

The term *hypocrites*, as used here,
describes people who do good
acts for appearances only—not
out of compassion or other good
motives. Their actions may be
good, but their motives are hollow.
The attention they may get is their
only reward, but God will reward
those who are sincere in their faith.

"A tree is identified by its fruit. If a tree is good, its fruit will be good. If a tree is bad, its fruit will be bad. You brood of snakes! How could evil men like you speak what is good and right? For whatever is in your heart determines what you say. A good person produces good things from the treasury of a good heart, and an evil person produces evil things from the treasury of an evil heart. And I tell you this, you must give an account on judgment day for every idle word you speak. The words you say will either acquit you or condemn you."

MATTHEW 12:33-37

REFLECTION

Jesus reminds us that what we say reveals what is in our hearts. What kinds of words come from your mouth? That is an indication of what is in your heart. You can't solve your heart problem, however, just by cleaning up your speech. You must allow the Holy Spirit to fill you with new attitudes and motives; then your speech will be cleansed at its source.

"It is what comes from inside that defiles you. For from within, out of a person's heart, come evil thoughts, sexual immorality, theft, murder, adultery, greed, wickedness, deceit, lustful desires, envy, slander, pride, and foolishness. All these vile things come from within; they are what defile you."

MARK 7:20-23

REFLECTION

An evil action begins with a single thought. Allowing our minds to dwell on lust, envy, hatred, or revenge will lead to sin. Don't defile yourself by focusing on evil.

Instead, follow Paul's advice in
Philippians 4:8 and think about
what is true, honorable, right,
pure, lovely, and admirable.

"No one lights a lamp and then hides
it or puts it under a basket. Instead,
a lamp is placed on a stand, where its
light can be seen by all who enter the
house.

"Your eye is a lamp that provides
light for your body. When your eye is
good, your whole body is filled with
light. But when it is bad, your body
is filled with darkness. Make sure
that the light you think you have is
not actually darkness. If you are filled
with light, with no dark corners, then
your whole life will be radiant, as
though a floodlight were filling you
with light."

Luke 11:33-36

REFLECTION

The lamp is Christ; the eye represents spiritual understanding and insight. Evil desires make the eye less sensitive and blot out the light of Christ's presence. If you have a hard time seeing God at work in the world and in your life, check your vision. Are any sinful desires blinding you to Christ?

True Worship

"Believe me, dear woman, the time is coming when it will no longer matter whether you worship the Father on this mountain or in Jerusalem. You Samaritans know very little about the one you worship, while we Jews know all about him, for salvation comes through the Jews. But the time is coming—indeed it's here now—when true worshipers will worship the Father in spirit and in truth. The Father is looking for those who will worship him that way. For God is Spirit, so those who worship him must worship in spirit and in truth."

JOHN 4:21-24

REFLECTION

"God is Spirit" means He is not a physical being limited to one place. He is present everywhere, and He can be worshiped anywhere, at any time. It is not where we worship that counts, but how we worship. Is your worship genuine and true? Do you have the Holy Spirit's help? How does the Holy Spirit help us worship? The Holy Spirit prays for us, teaches us the words of Christ, and tells us we are loved.

WARNINGS
OF JESUS

Warnings about False Teachers

"Beware of false prophets who come disguised as harmless sheep but are really vicious wolves. You can identify them by their fruit, that is, by the way they act. Can you pick grapes from thornbushes, or figs from thistles? A good tree produces good fruit, and a bad tree produces bad fruit. A good tree can't produce bad fruit, and a bad tree can't produce good fruit. So every tree that does not produce good fruit is chopped down and thrown into the fire. Yes, just as you can identify a tree by its fruit, so you can identify people by their actions.

"Not everyone who calls out to me, 'Lord! Lord!' will enter the Kingdom of Heaven. Only those who actually do the will of my Father in heaven will enter."

MATTHEW 7:15-21

REFLECTION

There were false prophets in Jesus' day, and we have them today. They are the leaders who are popular for telling people what they want to hear. Jesus says to beware of those whose words sound religious but who are motivated by money, fame, or power. You can tell who they are because in their teaching they minimize Christ and glorify themselves. Jesus said false teachers would come, and He warned His disciples, as He

warns us, not to listen to their
dangerous words.

"Don't let anyone mislead you, for
many will come in my name, claiming, 'I am the Messiah.' They will
deceive many. And you will hear of
wars and threats of wars, but don't
panic. Yes, these things must take
place, but the end won't follow
immediately. Nation will go to war
against nation, and kingdom against
kingdom. There will be famines and
earthquakes in many parts of the
world. But all this is only the first of
the birth pains, with more to come.

"Then you will be arrested,
persecuted, and killed. You will be
hated all over the world because
you are my followers. And many
will turn away from me and betray
and hate each other. And many false
prophets will appear and will deceive

many people. Sin will be rampant everywhere, and the love of many will grow cold. But the one who endures to the end will be saved."

MATTHEW 24:4-13

REFLECTION

The disciples asked Jesus for the sign of His coming and of the end of the age. Jesus' first response was "Don't let anyone mislead you." The fact is that whenever we look for signs, we become very susceptible to being deceived. There are many "false prophets" around with counterfeit signs of spiritual power and authority. The only sure way to keep from being deceived is to focus on Christ and His words. Don't look for special signs, and don't spend time looking at other people. Look at Christ.

Warnings about Hypocrisy

"When you fast, don't make it obvious, as the hypocrites do, for they try to look miserable and disheveled so people will admire them for their fasting. I tell you the truth, that is the only reward they will ever get. But when you fast, comb your hair and wash your face. Then no one will notice that you are fasting, except your Father, who knows what you do in private. And your Father, who sees everything, will reward you."

MATTHEW 6:16-18

Reflection

Fasting—going without food in order to spend time in prayer—is noble *and* difficult. It gives us time to pray, teaches self-discipline, reminds us that we can live with a lot less, and helps us appreciate God's gifts. Jesus was not condemning fasting, but hypocrisy—fasting in order to gain public approval. Many Pharisees voluntarily fasted twice a week to impress the people with their "holiness." Jesus commended acts of self-sacrifice done quietly and sincerely. He wanted people to adopt spiritual disciplines for the right reasons, not from a selfish desire for praise.

"The teachers of religious law and the Pharisees are the official interpreters of the law of Moses. So practice and obey whatever they tell you, but don't follow their example. For they don't practice what they teach. They crush people with unbearable religious demands and never lift a finger to ease the burden."

MATTHEW 23:2-4

REFLECTION

The Pharisees' traditions and their interpretations and applications of the laws had become as important to them as God's law itself. Their laws were not all bad—some were beneficial. Problems arose when the religious leaders (1) held that man-made rules were equal to God's laws, (2) told the people to obey these rules but did not

do so themselves, or (3) obeyed
the rules, not to honor God, but
to make themselves look good.
Usually Jesus did not condemn
what the Pharisees taught but
what they *were*—hypocrites.

"What sorrow awaits you teachers
of religious law and you Pharisees.
Hypocrites! For you shut the door
of the Kingdom of Heaven in
people's faces. You won't go in yourselves, and you don't let others enter
either. What sorrow awaits you
teachers of religious law and you
Pharisees. Hypocrites!"

MATTHEW 23:13-15

REFLECTION

Being a religious leader in
Jerusalem was very different
from being a pastor in a secular
society today. Israel's history,

culture, and daily life centered around its relationship with God. The religious leaders were the best known, most powerful, and most respected of all leaders. Jesus made these stinging accusations because the leaders' hunger for more power, money, and status had made them lose sight of God, and their blindness was spreading to the whole nation.

"Beware of these teachers of religious law! For they like to parade around in flowing robes and receive respectful greetings as they walk in the marketplaces. And how they love the seats of honor in the synagogues and the head table at banquets."

MARK 12:38-39

REFLECTION

Jesus warned against trying to make a good impression. These teachers of religious law were religious hypocrites who had no love for God. True followers of Christ are not distinguished by showy spirituality. Reading the Bible, praying in public, or following church rituals can be phony if the motive for doing them is to be noticed or honored. Let your actions be consistent with your beliefs. Live for Christ, even when no one is looking.

"**What sorrow awaits you teachers of religious law and you Pharisees. Hypocrites! For you are careful to tithe even the tiniest income from your herb gardens, but you ignore the** more important aspects of the law—justice, mercy, and faith. You should tithe, yes, but do not neglect the more important things. Blind guides! You strain your water so you won't accidentally swallow a gnat, but you swallow a camel!"

MATTHEW 23:23-24

REFLECTION

It's possible to obey the details of the laws but still be disobedient in our general behavior. For example, we could be very precise and faithful about giving 10 percent of our money to God but refuse to give one minute of our time in helping others. Tithing is important, but giving a tithe does not exempt us from fulfilling God's other directives.

"What sorrow awaits you teachers of religious law and you Pharisees. Hypocrites! For you are like white-washed tombs—beautiful on the outside but filled on the inside with dead people's bones and all sorts of impurity. Outwardly you look like righteous people, but inwardly your hearts are filled with hypocrisy and lawlessness."

MATTHEW 23:27-28

REFLECTION

Jesus condemned the Pharisees and religious leaders for outwardly appearing upright and holy but inwardly remaining full of corruption and greed. Living our Christianity merely as a show for others is like washing only the outside of a cup. When we are clean on the inside, our cleanliness on the outside won't be a sham.

Warnings of Persecution

"Look, I am sending you out as sheep among wolves. So be as shrewd as snakes and harmless as doves. But beware! For you will be handed over to the courts and will be flogged with whips in the synagogues. You will stand trial before governors and kings because you are my followers. But this will be your opportunity to tell the rulers and other unbelievers about me. When you are arrested, don't worry about how to respond or what to say. God will give you the right words at the right time. For it is not you who will be speaking—it will be the Spirit of your Father speaking through you.

"A brother will betray his brother to death, a father will betray his own child, and children will rebel against their parents and cause them to be killed. And all nations will hate you because you are my followers. But everyone who endures to the end will be saved. When you are persecuted in one town, flee to the next. I tell you the truth, the Son of Man will return before you have reached all the towns of Israel."

MATTHEW 10:16-23

REFLECTION

Enduring to the end is not a way to be saved but the evidence that a person is really committed to Jesus. Persistence is not a means to earn salvation; it is the by-product of a truly devoted life.

"This is my command: Love each other.

"If the world hates you, remember that it hated me first. The world would love you as one of its own if you belonged to it, but you are no longer part of the world. I chose you to come out of the world, so it hates you. Do you remember what I told you? 'A slave is not greater than the master.' Since they persecuted me, naturally they will persecute you. And if they had listened to me, they would listen to you. They will do all this to you because of me, for they have rejected the one who sent me."

JOHN 15:17-21

REFLECTION

Christians will get plenty of hatred from the world; from each other we need love and support. Do you allow small problems to get in the way of loving other believers? Jesus commands that you love them, and He will give you the strength to do it.

"The time is coming—indeed it's here now—when you will be scattered, each one going his own way, leaving me alone. Yet I am not alone because the Father is with me. I have told you all this so that you may have peace in me. Here on earth you will have many trials and sorrows. But take heart, because I have overcome the world."

JOHN 16:32-33

REFLECTION

In these verses Jesus told His disciples to take courage. In spite of the inevitable struggles they would face, they would not be alone. Jesus does not abandon us to our struggles either. If we remember that the ultimate victory has already been won, we can claim the peace of Christ in the most troublesome times.

Warnings of Coming Judgment

"On judgment day many will say to me, 'Lord! Lord! We prophesied in your name and cast out demons in your name and performed many miracles in your name.' But I will reply, 'I never knew you. Get away from me, you who break God's laws.'"

MATTHEW 7:22-23

REFLECTION

Judgment Day is the final day of reckoning when God will settle all accounts, judging sin and rewarding faith.

"The Kingdom of Heaven is like a farmer who planted good seed in his field. But that night as the workers slept, his enemy came and planted weeds among the wheat, then slipped away. When the crop began to grow and produce grain, the weeds also grew.

"The farmer's workers went to him and said, 'Sir, the field where you planted that good seed is full of weeds! Where did they come from?'

"'An enemy has done this!' the farmer exclaimed.

"'Should we pull out the weeds?' they asked.

"'No,' he replied, 'you'll uproot the wheat if you do. Let both grow together until the harvest. Then I will tell the harvesters to sort out the weeds, tie them into bundles, and burn them, and to put the wheat in the barn.'"

MATTHEW 13:24-30

REFLECTION

The young weeds and the young blades of wheat can't be separated until they are grown and ready for harvest. Weeds (unbelievers) and wheat (believers) must live side by side in this world. God allows unbelievers to remain for a while, just as a farmer allows weeds to remain in his field so the surrounding wheat isn't uprooted with them. At the harvest, however, the weeds will be uprooted and thrown away. God's harvest (judgment) of all people is coming. We are to make ourselves ready by making sure that our faith is sincere.

"The Kingdom of Heaven is like a fishing net that was thrown into the water and caught fish of every

kind. When the net was full, they dragged it up onto the shore, sat down, and sorted the good fish into crates, but threw the bad ones away. That is the way it will be at the end of the world. The angels will come and separate the wicked people from the righteous, throwing the wicked into the fiery furnace, where there will be weeping and gnashing of teeth. Do you understand all these things?"

MATTHEW 13:47-51

REFLECTION

The parable of the fishing net has the same meaning as the parable of the wheat and weeds. We are to obey God and tell others about His grace and goodness, but we cannot discern who is part of the Kingdom of Heaven and who is not. This sorting will be done at the Last Judgment by those infinitely more qualified than we.

"When the Son of Man comes in his glory, and all the angels with him, then he will sit upon his glorious throne. All the nations will be gathered in his presence, and he will separate the people as a shepherd separates the sheep from the goats. He will place the sheep at his right hand and the goats at his left.

"Then the King will say to those on his right, 'Come, you who are blessed by my Father, inherit the Kingdom prepared for you from the creation of the world. For I was hungry, and you fed me. I was thirsty, and you gave me a drink. I was a stranger, and you invited me into your home. I was naked, and you gave me clothing. I was sick, and you cared for me. I was in prison, and you visited me.'

"Then these righteous ones will reply, 'Lord, when did we ever see you hungry and feed you? Or thirsty and give you something to drink? Or a stranger and show you hospitality? Or naked and give you clothing? When did we ever see you sick or in prison and visit you?'

"And the King will say, 'I tell you the truth, when you did it to one of the least of these my brothers and sisters, you were doing it to me!'

"Then the King will turn to those on the left and say, 'Away with you, you cursed ones, into the eternal fire prepared for the devil and his demons. For I was hungry, and you didn't feed me. I was thirsty, and you didn't give me a drink. I was a stranger, and you didn't invite me into your home. I was naked, and you didn't give me clothing. I was sick and in prison, and you didn't visit me.'

"Then they will reply, 'Lord, when did we ever see you hungry or thirsty or a stranger or naked or sick or in prison, and not help you?'

"And he will answer, 'I tell you the truth, when you refused to help the least of these my brothers and sisters, you were refusing to help me.'

"And they will go away into eternal punishment, but the righteous will go into eternal life."

MATTHEW 25:31-46

REFLECTION

God will separate His obedient followers from pretenders and unbelievers. The real evidence of our belief is the way we act. To treat all persons we encounter as if they were Jesus is no easy task.

What we do for others demonstrates what we really think about Jesus' words to us: feed the hungry, give the homeless a place to stay, look after the sick. How well do your actions separate you from pretenders and unbelievers?

Signs of the End Times

"Don't let anyone mislead you, for many will come in my name, claiming, 'I am the Messiah.' They will deceive many. And you will hear of wars and threats of wars, but don't panic. Yes, these things must take place, but the end won't follow immediately. Nation will go to war against nation, and kingdom against kingdom. There will be earthquakes in many parts of the world, as well as famines. But this is only the first of the birth pains, with more to come.

"When these things begin to

happen, watch out! You will be handed over to the local councils and beaten in the synagogues. You will stand trial before governors and kings because you are my followers. But this will be your opportunity to tell them about me. For the Good News must first be preached to all nations. But when you are arrested and stand trial, don't worry in advance about what to say. Just say what God tells you at that time, for it is not you who will be speaking, but the Holy Spirit."

MARK 13:5-11

REFLECTION

What are the signs of the end times? There have been people in every generation since Christ's resurrection claiming to know exactly when Jesus would return. No one has been right yet, however, because Christ will return on God's timetable, not ours. Jesus predicted that before His return, many believers would be misled by false teachers claiming to have revelations from God.

According to Scripture, one clear sign of Christ's return will be His unmistakable appearance in the clouds, which will be seen by all people. In other words, you do not have to wonder whether a certain person is the Messiah or whether these are the "end times." When Jesus returns, *you will know* beyond a doubt, because it will be evident to all true believers. Beware of groups who claim special knowledge of Christ's return, because no one knows when that time will be. Be cautious about saying, "This

is it!" but be bold in your total
commitment to have your heart
and life ready for Christ's return.

"A brother will betray his brother to
death, a father will betray his own
child, and children will rebel against
their parents and cause them to be
killed. And everyone will hate you
because you are my followers. But the
one who endures to the end will be
saved."

MARK 13:12-13

REFLECTION

To believe in Jesus and endure
to the end will take perseverance
because our faith will be challenged and opposed. Severe trials
will sift true Christians from fair-
weather believers. Enduring to
the end does not earn salvation

for us but marks us as already saved. The assurance of our salvation will keep us strong in times of persecution.

"The day is coming when you will see the sacrilegious object that causes desecration standing where he should not be." (Reader, pay attention!) "Then those in Judea must flee to the hills. A person out on the deck of a roof must not go down into the house to pack. A person out in the field must not return even to get a coat. How terrible it will be for pregnant women and for nursing mothers in those days. And pray that your flight will not be in winter. For there will be greater anguish in those days than at any time since God created the world. And it will never be so great again. In fact, unless the Lord shortens that time of calamity, not a single person will survive. But for the sake of his chosen ones he has shortened those days.

"Then if anyone tells you, 'Look, here is the Messiah,' or 'There he is,' don't believe it. For false messiahs and false prophets will rise up and perform signs and wonders so as to deceive, if possible, even God's chosen ones. Watch out! I have warned you about this ahead of time!

"At that time, after the anguish of those days,

> the sun will be darkened,
> the moon will give no light,
> the stars will fall from the sky,
> and the powers in the heavens
> will be shaken.

Then everyone will see the Son of Man coming on the clouds with great power and glory. And he will send out his angels to gather his chosen ones from all over the world—from the farthest ends of the earth and heaven.

"Now learn a lesson from the fig tree. When its branches bud and its leaves begin to sprout, you know that summer is near. In the same way, when you see all these things taking place, you can know that his return is very near, right at the door. I tell you the truth, this generation will not pass from the scene before all these things take place. Heaven and earth will disappear, but my words will never disappear."

MARK 13:14-31

REFLECTION

In Jesus' day the world seemed concrete, dependable, and permanent. The truth that heaven and earth will disappear is all that much more believable in our age of nuclear power and terrorism. Jesus tells us, however, that even though the earth will pass away, the truth of His words will never be changed or abolished. God and His Word provide the only stability in our unstable world. How shortsighted people are who spend all their time and energy learning about this temporary world and accumulating its possessions, while neglecting the Bible and its eternal truths!

"No one knows the day or hour when these things will happen, not even the angels in heaven or the Son himself. Only the Father knows. And since you don't know when that time will come, be on guard! Stay alert!"

MARK 13:32-33

REFLECTION

When Jesus said that even He did not know the time of the end, He was affirming His humanity. Of course God the Father knows the time, and Jesus and the Father are one. But when Jesus became a man, He voluntarily gave up the unlimited use of His divine attributes.

The emphasis of this verse is not on Jesus' lack of knowledge but rather on the fact that no one knows. It is God the Father's secret to be revealed when He wills. No one can predict by Scripture or science the exact day of Jesus' return. Jesus is teaching that preparation, not calculation, is needed.

OTHER
ILLUSTRATIONS
JESUS USED

Jesus' Radical Message

"No one tears a piece of cloth from a new garment and uses it to patch an old garment. For then the new garment would be ruined, and the new patch wouldn't even match the old garment.

"And no one puts new wine into old wineskins. For the new wine would burst the wineskins, spilling the wine and ruining the skins. New wine must be stored in new wineskins. But no one who drinks the old wine seems to want the new wine. 'The old is just fine,' they say."

LUKE 5:36-39

REFLECTION

Wineskins were goatskins sewn
together at the edges to form
watertight bags. Because new
wine expands as it ages, it had to
be put in new, pliable wineskins.
A used skin, having become
more rigid, would burst and spill
the wine. Like old wineskins,
the Pharisees were too rigid to
accept Jesus, who could not be
contained in their traditions or
rules. Christianity required new
approaches, new traditions, new
structures. Our church programs
and ministries should not be
so structured that they have no
room for a fresh touch of the
Spirit, a new method, or a new
idea. We, too, must be careful
that our hearts do not become so
rigid that they prevent us from

accepting new ways of thinking that Christ brings. We need
to keep our hearts pliable so we
can accept Jesus' life-changing
message.

Ready for the Kingdom

"The coming of the Son of Man can be illustrated by the story of a man going on a long trip. When he left home, he gave each of his slaves instructions about the work they were to do, and he told the gatekeeper to watch for his return. You, too, must keep watch! For you don't know when the master of the household will return—in the evening, at midnight, before dawn, or at daybreak. Don't let him find you sleeping when he arrives without warning. I say to you what I say to everyone: Watch for him!"

MARK 13:34-37

REFLECTION

How should we live while we
wait for Christ's return? (1) We
are not to be misled by confus-
ing claims or speculative interpretations of what will happen.
(2) We should not be afraid to
tell people about Christ, despite
what they might say or do to
us. (3) We must stand firm by
faith and not be surprised by
persecution. (4) We must be
morally alert, obedient to the
commands for living found in
God's Word. These words were
not given to promote discus-
sions on prophetic timetables
but to stimulate right living
for God in a world that largely
ignores Him.

"The Kingdom of Heaven will be like ten bridesmaids who took their lamps and went to meet the bridegroom. Five of them were foolish, and five were wise. The five who were foolish didn't take enough olive oil for their lamps, but the other five were wise enough to take along extra oil. When the bridegroom was delayed, they all became drowsy and fell asleep.

"At midnight they were roused by the shout, 'Look, the bridegroom is coming! Come out and meet him!'

"All the bridesmaids got up and prepared their lamps. Then the five foolish ones asked the others, 'Please give us some of your oil because our lamps are going out.'

"But the others replied, 'We don't have enough for all of us. Go to a shop and buy some for yourselves.'

"But while they were gone to buy

oil, the bridegroom came. Then those who were ready went in with him to the marriage feast, and the door was locked. Later, when the other five bridesmaids returned, they stood outside, calling, 'Lord! Lord! Open the door for us!'

"But he called back, 'Believe me, I don't know you!'

"So you, too, must keep watch! For you do not know the day or hour of my return."

MATTHEW 25:1-13

REFLECTION

In this parable, Jesus clarifies what it means to be ready for His return and how to live until He comes. We learn that every person is responsible for his or her own spiritual condition. When Jesus returns to take His people to heaven, we must be

ready. Spiritual preparation cannot be bought or borrowed at
the last minute. Our relationship with God must be our own.

"The Kingdom of Heaven can be illustrated by the story of a king who prepared a great wedding feast for his son.
When the banquet was ready, he sent
his servants to notify those who were
invited. But they all refused to come!

"So he sent other servants to tell
them, 'The feast has been prepared.
The bulls and fattened cattle have
been killed, and everything is ready.
Come to the banquet!' But the guests
he had invited ignored them and
went their own way, one to his farm,
another to his business. Others seized
his messengers and insulted them and
killed them.

"The king was furious, and he sent
out his army to destroy the murderers

and burn their town. And he said to his servants, 'The wedding feast is ready, and the guests I invited aren't worthy of the honor. Now go out to the street corners and invite everyone you see.' So the servants brought in everyone they could find, good and bad alike, and the banquet hall was filled with guests.

"But when the king came in to meet the guests, he noticed a man who wasn't wearing the proper clothes for a wedding. 'Friend,' he asked, 'how is it that you are here without wedding clothes?' But the man had no reply. Then the king said to his aides, 'Bind his hands and feet and throw him into the outer darkness, where there will be weeping and gnashing of teeth.'

"For many are called, but few are chosen."

MATTHEW 22:2-14

REFLECTION

In Jesus' culture, two invitations were expected when banquets were given. The first asked the guests to attend; the second announced that all was ready. In this story the king invited his guests three times, and each time they rejected his invitation. God wants us to join Him at His banquet, which will last for eternity. That's why He sends us invitations again and again. Have you accepted His invitation?

The Last Will Be First

"The Kingdom of Heaven is like the landowner who went out early one morning to hire workers for his vineyard. He agreed to pay the normal daily wage and sent them out to work.

"At nine o'clock in the morning he was passing through the marketplace and saw some people standing around doing nothing. So he hired them, telling them he would pay them whatever was right at the end of the day. So they went to work in the vineyard. At noon and again at three o'clock he did the same thing.

"At five o'clock that afternoon he was in town again and saw some more people standing around. He asked them, 'Why haven't you been working today?'

"They replied, 'Because no one hired us.'

"The landowner told them, 'Then go out and join the others in my vineyard.'

"That evening he told the foreman to call the workers in and pay them, beginning with the last workers first. When those hired at five o'clock were paid, each received a full day's wage. When those hired first came to get their pay, they assumed they would receive more. But they, too, were paid a day's wage. When they received their pay, they protested to the owner, 'Those people worked only one hour, and yet you've paid them just as much as you paid us who worked all day in the scorching heat.'

"He answered one of them, 'Friend, I haven't been unfair! Didn't you agree to work all day for the usual wage? Take your money and go. I wanted to pay this last worker the same as you. Is it against the law for me to do what I want with my money? Should you be jealous because I am kind to others?'

"So those who are last now will be first then, and those who are first will be last."

MATTHEW 20:1-16

REFLECTION

Jesus further clarified the membership rules of the Kingdom of Heaven: entrance is by God's grace alone. In this parable, God is the landowner and believers are the workers. This parable speaks especially to those who feel superior because of heritage or position, to those who feel superior because they have spent so much time with Christ, and to new believers as reassurance of God's grace.

The Rejection of Jesus

"A man planted a vineyard. He built a wall around it, dug a pit for pressing out the grape juice, and built a lookout tower. Then he leased the vineyard to tenant farmers and moved to another country. At the time of the grape harvest, he sent one of his servants to collect his share of the crop. But the farmers grabbed the servant, beat him up, and sent him back empty-handed. The owner then sent another servant, but they insulted him and beat him over the head. The next servant he sent was killed. Others he sent were either beaten or killed, until there was only one left—his son whom he loved dearly. The owner finally sent him, thinking, 'Surely they will respect my son.'

"But the tenant farmers said to one another, 'Here comes the heir to this estate. Let's kill him and get the estate for ourselves!' So they grabbed him and murdered him and threw his body out of the vineyard.

"What do you suppose the owner of the vineyard will do?" Jesus asked. "I'll tell you—he will come and kill those farmers and lease the vineyard to others."

MARK 12:1-9

REFLECTION

In this parable, the man who planted the vineyard is God; the vineyard is the nation Israel; the tenant farmers are Israel's religious leaders; the servants are the prophets and priests who remained faithful to God; the son is Jesus; and the others are the Gentiles. The religious leaders not only frustrated their nation's purpose but also killed those who were trying to fulfill it. They were so jealous and possessive that they ignored the welfare of the very people they were supposed to be bringing to God. By telling this story, Jesus exposed the religious leaders' plot to kill Him and warned that their sins would be punished.

Wise Stewardship

"The Kingdom of Heaven can be illustrated by the story of a man going on a long trip. He called together his servants and entrusted his money to them while he was gone. He gave five bags of silver to one, two bags of silver to another, and one bag of silver to the last—dividing it in proportion to their abilities. He then left on his trip.

"The servant who received the five bags of silver began to invest the money and earned five more. The servant with two bags of silver also went to work and earned two more. But the servant who received the one bag of silver dug a hole in the ground and hid the master's money.

"After a long time their master returned from his trip and called them to give an account of how they had used his money. The servant to whom he had entrusted the five bags of silver came forward with five more and said, 'Master, you gave me five bags of silver to invest, and I have earned five more.'

"The master was full of praise. 'Well done, my good and faithful servant. You have been faithful in handling this small amount, so now I will give you many more responsibilities. Let's celebrate together!'

"The servant who had received the two bags of silver came forward and said, 'Master, you gave me two bags of silver to invest, and I have earned two more.'

"The master said, 'Well done, my good and faithful servant. You have been faithful in handling this small amount, so now I will give you many more responsibilities. Let's celebrate together!'

"Then the servant with the one bag of silver came and said, 'Master, I knew you were a harsh man, harvesting crops you didn't plant and gathering crops you didn't cultivate. I was afraid I would lose your money, so I hid it in the earth. Look, here is your money back.'

"But the master replied, 'You wicked and lazy servant! If you knew I harvested crops I didn't plant and gathered crops I didn't cultivate, why didn't you deposit my money in the bank? At least I could have gotten some interest on it.'

"Then he ordered, 'Take the money from this servant, and give it to the one with the ten bags of silver. To those who use well what they are given, even more will be given, and they will have an abundance. But from those who do nothing, even what little they have will be taken away. Now throw this useless servant into outer darkness, where there will be weeping and gnashing of teeth.'"

MATTHEW 25:14-30

REFLECTION

This parable describes the consequences of two attitudes toward Christ's return. The person who diligently prepares for it by investing his or her time and talents to serve God will be rewarded. The person who has no heart for the work of the Kingdom will be punished. God rewards faithfulness. Those who bear no fruit for God's Kingdom cannot expect to be treated the same as those who are faithful.

"There was a certain rich man who had a manager handling his affairs. One day a report came that the manager was wasting his employer's money. So the employer called him in and said, 'What's this I hear about you? Get your report in order, because you are going to be fired.'

"The manager thought to himself, 'Now what? My boss has fired me. I don't have the strength to dig ditches, and I'm too proud to beg. Ah, I know

how to ensure that I'll have plenty
of friends who will give me a home
when I am fired.'

"So he invited each person who
owed money to his employer to come
and discuss the situation. He asked
the first one, 'How much do you
owe him?' The man replied, 'I owe
him 800 gallons of olive oil.' So the
manager told him, 'Take the bill and
quickly change it to 400 gallons.'

"'And how much do you owe my
employer?' he asked the next man.
'I owe him 1,000 bushels of wheat,'
was the reply. 'Here,' the manager
said, 'take the bill and change it to
800 bushels.'

"The rich man had to admire the
dishonest rascal for being so shrewd.
And it is true that the children of this
world are more shrewd in dealing with
the world around them than are the

children of the light. Here's the lesson: use your worldly resources to benefit others and make friends. Then, when your earthly possessions are gone, they will welcome you to an eternal home.

"If you are faithful in little things, you will be faithful in large ones. But if you are dishonest in little things, you won't be honest with greater responsibilities. And if you are untrustworthy about worldly wealth, who will trust you with the true riches of heaven? And if you are not faithful with other people's things, why should you be trusted with things of your own?

"No one can serve two masters. For you will hate one and love the other; you will be devoted to one and despise the other. You cannot serve both God and money."

LUKE 16:1-13

Reflection

We are to make wise use of the financial opportunities we have, not to earn heaven but to help people find Christ. If we use our money to help those in need or to help others find Christ, our earthly investment will bring eternal benefit. When we obey God's will, the unselfish use of possessions will follow.

Notes

Notes

Notes

Notes

Notes

Notes

Notes

Notes

Notes

Notes

Notes

Notes

Notes